WORD
RECREATIONS

WORD RECREATIONS

GAMES AND DIVERSIONS FROM
WORD WAYS

A. Ross Eckler

DOVER PUBLICATIONS, INC.
NEW YORK

Published in Canada by General Publishing Company, Ltd., 30 Lesmill Road, Don Mills, Toronto, Ontario.
Published in the United Kingdom by Constable and Company, Ltd., 10 Orange Street, London WC2H 7EG.

Word Recreations is a new anthology of articles, by A. Ross Eckler and others, which appeared in *Word Ways* magazine. The book also contains a substantial amount of previously unpublished material prepared by the author.

International Standard Book Number: 0-486-23854-7
Library of Congress Catalog Card Number: 79-51884

Manufactured in the United States of America
Dover Publications, Inc.
180 Varick Street
New York, N.Y. 10014

CONTENTS

INTRODUCTION   1

OULIPO   4
    Transposition Poetry
    Word Substitution

LIPOGRAMS   10
    Mary Had a Lipogram
    Poems in Praise of English Phonology

HIDDEN MESSAGES   15
    A Readable Polyphonic Cipher
    Penney Puzzles

WORD NETWORKS   24

TRANSPOSALS   33
    Long Well-Mixed Transposals
    State Name Transposals

THE TWO RAVENS   44
    The Acrostic Raven
    The Heteroliteral Raven

LINGUISTS AT PLAY   51
    Superl
    The Language Game

WORD SQUARES   56
    Six-by-Six Double Word Squares
    The Search for a Ten-by-Ten Word Square
    Cubism

HIGH-SCORING SCRABBLE   64

PLACE NAME WORDPLAY   69
    American Place Names
    A State Name Chain
    State Name Charades
    Piddletrenthide
    English Place Names

BRITISH WORD PUZZLES   84
    Eighteenth-Century Puzzles
    Nineteenth-Century Puzzles

PANGRAMS   100
    Pangram Variations
    3330 Pangrams
    Literary Pangrams

PENCIL-AND-PAPER WORD GAMES   108

TEN LOGOTOPIAN LINGOS   123

THE LAST WORD   133

INTRODUCTION

People have been playing with words since the time of the ancient Greeks. However, wordplay was not clearly perceived to be a separate field of study, somewhat analogous to recreational mathematics, until the publication of Dmitri A. Borgmann's book, Language on Vacation, in 1965, which systematically examined many different types of wordplay. In this book, he rehabilitated an old word to describe the new field; he proposed that logology, once defined as the "science of words" and illustrated by two nineteenth-century quotations in the Oxford English Dictionary, be a synonym for "recreational linguistics". In 1968 he founded the quarterly magazine Word Ways, the Journal of Recreational Linguistics to provide a form for reporting new discoveries in logology, and served as its editor for the first year (Word Ways is currently edited and published at Spring Valley Road, Morristown, New Jersey 07960). There is little doubt that he has done more to bring the subject of logology to general attention than any other individual.

What, then, is logology? Formed at the intersection of three older fields of intellectual endeavor -- academic linguistics, poetic and literary experimentation, and word puzzles -- its boundaries are somewhat indefinite. Corresponding to these fields, logological concepts can be presented in three different ways: as an individual example (what plural ending in S is converted to a singular word with a second S?), as a literary constraint (a poem or novel written without the letter E), or as a piece of linguistic research (what collection of letters can be rearranged in the most different ways to form words?). Logology can be defined by its subject matter as developed in Language on Vacation and Word Ways. The following brief taxonomy of logology's core may give a hint of its riches (a few examples are given in parentheses).

A. Patterns of Words

    1. Single-word patterns
        a. Patterns involving all letters of the word (palindromes: DEIFIED; tautonyms: MURMUR)
        b. Patterns involving fragments of a word
            (1) anchored fragments (words starting and ending with specified letters: AreA, AraB, ... , ZizZ)
            (2) floating fragments (each bigram: bazAAr, dAB, ... , jaZZ; vowels in all orders: fAcEtIOUs, sEqUOIA, ...)
        c. Patterns involving distributions of letters in words (words with no repeated letters: AMBIDEXTROUSLY; words with each letter appearing twice: INTESTINES)
        d. Patterns involving the number of letters in a word (long words)

    2. Multiple-word patterns
       a. Pangrams (CWM, NTH, FJORD, QUIZ, VEX, BALKS, GYP)
       b. Partially overlapping word groups (CAN, COT, ATE, ONE)
       c. Word squares

    3. Patterns dependent on alphabetic order
       a. Letter order only (letters in order: ALMOST; in reverse
          order: SPONGE)
       b. Letter-scoring A = 1, B = 2, ... (CAN 3,1,14 to DO 4,15)

B. Operations on Words

    1. Elementary operations
       a. Deletions (beheadments and curtailments: WHEAT-HEAT-
          EAT-AT-T; charitable words: SEAT - EAT, SAT, SET, SEA)
       b. Insertions (hospitable words: RAN - BRAN, ROAN, RAIN,
          RANK)

    2. Single deletion plus single insertion
       a. Delete letter at end, insert letter at start (word stairs:
          TSAR-SARI-ARID-RIDE ...)
       b. Delete letter, insert another letter at same place (word
          ladders: SHARE-SPARE-SPARK ...)
       c. Delete letter, insert same letter at different place in word
          (leads to transposals: OLIVE to VOILE)

    3. Deletion or insertion combined with transposition (transdeletion:
       A-AT-TAN-NEAT-THANE-... ; word progression: NOLARECI -
       LOAN, ORAL, REAL, CARE, RICE)

C. Relationship Between Sight and Sound in Words (homonyms: BARE-
    BEAR; silent letters: Aisle, Bdelium, ... , rendeZvous; add let-
    ters and reduce syllables: AGED-STAGED)

    Logology deals with words -- but what is a word? This question is
crucial to logological studies, for the answer to a problem (even the
solvability of a problem!) depends upon the words that are allowed;
for an example, see the chapter "The Last Word". It is tempting to
say that a word exists if examples of it can be found in English-language
texts, but this definition is of no practical value, for it is impossible
to search for the occurrence of a rare but possibly-plausible sequence
of letters. Recognizing that this is the method used by dictionary-
compilers to decide on their entries, one can define a word as a sequence of letters which appears in boldface type in one or more specified dictionaries. However, many well-known words are not found
there. Derived forms, such as noun plurals, verb past tenses and
gerunds, do not usually appear in boldface, but these must certainly
be allowed. Sometimes dictionaries do not include words in common
use -- Dmitri Borgmann cites the examples of ex-wife, uncashed and
duty-bound in Language on Vacation. As these words illustrate, one
must also decide whether to allow words that have internal punctuation
such as apostrophes or hyphens. Should two-word combinations found

in dictionaries (such as <u>chop suey</u>) be regarded as a single word for the purpose of such operations as transposition? If not, should individual words which appear only in multiword phrases (such as <u>suey</u>) be allowed instead?

Where does one draw the line between words and non-words as one considers rarer words? Should highly specialized words such as long chemical names, used by few people, be allowed? In the limit, one must deal with the nonce-word, invented by an author for a specific occasion and never seen elsewhere (see James Joyce for examples). Since words form a continuous spectrum of usage, it is hard to draw firm or meaningful demarcation lines.

The same questions arise when one goes back in time, to consider words once used by English speakers and writers but now obsolete. How far back into the Anglo-Saxon origins of the language should one go for examples? When does a word cease to exist, if ever?

Should place names, personal names or surnames be allowed as words? Many of these (<u>Detroit</u>, <u>Linda</u>, <u>Eisenhower</u>) are extremely well-known; again, it is <u>hard to draw a line between</u> admissible and inadmissible words. New problems arise: American place names seem reasonable enough, but should one also allow foreign place names which appear in English-language texts? It seems hard to deny the existence of a word such as <u>Budapest</u>, but once this is admitted should one also allow a tiny Albanian village? Rare surnames have the added problem of referencing -- there is no comprehensive list of published surnames, and examples cited in telephone directories may vanish in later editions.

As mentioned earlier, one can often locate non-dictionary words through reasoning by analogy. Should this reasoning be allowed free rein to construct logical "words" that may well have never appeared in literature? For example, the citation plural of a word is often encountered ("there are three 'verys' in this paragraph"); can <u>any</u> word be so pluralized? What about superlatives of rare adjectives, such as <u>intensivest</u>? Or the indiscriminate addition of prefixes or suffixes, such as <u>yuccalike</u> (which appears in a definition in Webster's Second Edition, under <u>sotol</u>)? Many questions of this sort can be raised to challenge one's conception of a word, and there are no easy answers.

OULIPO

OuLiPo, an acronym for Ouvroir de Litterature Potentielle, is a group of about twenty mathematicians and writers who meet once a month in Paris to present and discuss their inventions of novel constrictive forms. The name can be approximately translated to mean "workshop of potential literature". More precisely, ouvroir used to denote a place where well-to-do ladies would gather to sew or knit clothes for the poor; the word was adopted by OuLiPo to indicate, with self-deprecating irony, the communal, beneficial nature of the organization's labors.

OuLiPo was founded in 1960 by Francois LeLionnais and Raymond Queneau, men who shared an encyclopedic turn of mind, a passionate interest in new uses of language, and what one of them has called "mathematical gluttony". LeLionnais is, among other things, France's foremost authority on chess problems, and Queneau (who died in the autumn of 1976) was a novelist and poet of the very first rank, perhaps best known for his novel Zazie dans le Metro and his Elements of Style (a trivial anecdote told in 99 different ways). Both men often stated that for them the transposition of mathematical structures to literature was the most fruitful method of creating new means of expression. Their initiative gave their group a mathematical orientation that is fundamental, one that exerts an influence even on those members who are (to their regret) innocent of advanced mathematics. Most of its present membership is French, although it includes an Australian, a Belgian, an Italian, and an expatriate American novelist, Harry Mathews of Paris, France, the source of much of the information in this chapter.

Much of their work, unfortunately, is accessible only to the person familiar with French. In 1973, the group published a paperback, La Litterature Potentielle (Collection "Idees", Gallimard, Paris), which describes many of their activities, with examples. Some of their wordplay is a French-language version of well-known English-language constrictive forms: Georges Perec, one of their most prolific members, has published both a 5000-letter palindrome and a lipogrammatic novel omitting the letter E, La Disparition (Denoel, Paris, 1969); an elaborate, funny story of unbelievable virtuosity, it exceeds Wright's Gadsby in length and no doubt in literary quality. (When the book was reviewed, some critics failed to notice that it was a lipogram!)

Other OuLiPo wordplay is more unusual. This chapter samples the OuLiPo output, selecting those types of literary constraint for which English-language examples can be provided.

Transposition Poetry

Perec has published a series of poems consisting of words formed out of successive rearrangements of the eleven letters ULCERATIONS endlessly repeated. Perhaps the nearest analogue to this in English wordplay is the technique developed by James Rambo of Palo Alto, California, who takes a well-known short phrase and rearranges its letters many times to form a series of stanzas. In the following poem, the last line contains the original phrase.

An End to the Beginning	One who gets far often hurries, dares all. Rash and resolute, the legions offer war. We, the sane, hold fast anger is foul error. A fresh war? Not for us, the old line agrees.
The Telephone	A thrall aged sureness on or off the wire. No real news, age frets, dials for the hour. Forage there furnishes a lone last word. All so finger, rouse death for the answer.
A Word for the Weary	All, I one, share these words for great fun. He, she, all forage, for words entertain us. I rather less feel a word-hunt goes on far. Hell, word-sense tires after an hour, a fog.
Time to Go	Now a rash little dare, sheer ego runs off. Oh foul show, a fiend rearranges letters! Farewell's tough fare; sir, end a short one. Last for "so long" -- rather, "auf wiedersehen".
Sunset	The sunless learn, gather wood for a fire. Rest; fore sounds of night are all we hear. Eternal shadows gather for us, lone fire. Nor life redrawn, the ash flares, goes out.
Varietal Sin	All sin not greed, fewer shout for a share. Sloth was often a danger for her leisure. She no good herself, a flatterer was ruin. An auto-da-fe, hellfire, shows gents error.
Dry Heat	Sins held are felt rough water of reason. As for guilt, flesh errs on, a weed on earth. Regard hell's sauna, note it for fresh woe. Roar! God hears when one suffers a little.
After the Fall	Hade's offer here: tulle or satin rags now! Sinful feathered gowns or hats are lore. So she wore neat snug Dior after her fall. For a hold, Satan relies on furs we get her.

The Fancy House	Trade's fine for whole house, errant gals. Whore's rule: falter not, sin, forge ahead. Dollars are her fortune, the wages of sin. Harlots flourish, we nod, earn great fees.
A Simple Wedding?	Her wall near, he toots, offers a snug ride. At hand father, i.e. gun, follows, sees error. "Oh foul sinner," he roars, "get wed real fast!" Whole affair's star shotgun lore ere end.
The Tenor of the Times	Song, hero, lures a fan; set the world afire! Assure few for all noted tenors are high. Dolors we agree, hale tenors huff, strain. Worse, heroines fall, get tenors. Ah, fraud!
Paint	Galleries show off our arts, the end near. The sheer range -- it's a wonder for all of us. None were realists, half so fourth-grade. No art for age is there; elders howl, "Snafu!"
Shoddy Advice	New shoes are tortures affording a hell. Oh suffer on -- we all are shoestring trade. Dr. Hiss worn, are grateful feet soon hale? Hurl no free shoe. Forget it, wear sandals.
The Morning Paper	Rise, read news for "A shot rang out -- he fell!" Rule rote, the gals read for fashion news. The lure we are for -- ads for things on sale. All are readers for who's got the funnies?
A New Vein	One rash turn was the feel of Sierra gold. Few shall dig, one far era, nurse the roots. Shun life? Slots were arranged for Tahoe. Lo, the Sierra was fresh golden fortune.
Adventure	Learn great fashion for us: see the world! Assured whole, I sneer, at length roar off. I hog all, see a new forest or fresh tundra. A wrangler, friends, at the house of lores.
Fuel for What?	No, Rolls, we horde gas; there Fiats are fun. Near shortages of fuel hinder low rates. We furnish or store gas all need for heat. Senators wangled fuel for sheer hot air.
Fauna	Near sol hot, the unreal giraffes drowse. Lions roared at a hunger for sweet flesh. Tigers, so feral, shadow fare -- lone hunter. A wolf forges on, treasures the hard line.

Reno Casino

Slots here are woe for the girls -- and fun.
As fortune frowns she'll go, retire ahead.
Suffer, fal; win or lose, Reno has the trade.
These dollars! He's at Reno for fun, I wager.

Trackless
Wastes

No S. R. O. , we urge the real life -- far hot sands.
Fans so far, we'll rough it here on a desert.
Near our rash desert hotel was fine golf.
Green fees follow the torrid Sahara sun!

Chain
Reaction

Hash's free? Aw, let's go out for real dinner.
Our Shraffts here all great, we soon dine.
Well, restaurants are seen high for food.
Gosh, we had filets rare -- no real fortune.

Another
Battle

Near free foods, a lush girl won't eat hers.
We shall forego rashers, rue non-fat diet.
Need a law of loss? Shun the refrigerator!
Darn ragouts are sheer follies; heft won.

Trapped!

She leers awhirl, attunes range for food.
Date falls for her wise snare, too -- hunger!
Her trial souffle earns the answer, "Good!"
Lean, so grateful, he weds her for rations.

From Bladder
to Worse

Here gallons of tea sure drown this fare.
Sad, for the sheer unreason of it all grew.
The slosh offers natural wonder, I agree.
Tea worth renal agonies, holders suffer.

Wraith
Relations

Ghouls, risen, feed on raw flesh -- or a treat.
Ah, warn self, eidolons gesture for heart.
Fine or fare! Who needs later slur a ghost?
A groan fed terror; the fuss is Halloween.

Dogs and
Their Fleas

Fleas who range on a red setter flourish.
Show heart, terrier, a dog's lone flea's -- fun?
Hounds feel fleas, root, gnaw their rears.
Herein the rest dug also for war on fleas.

So Much
for Fish

Raw shellfish, true, are one strange food.
Hear, larder? Sense fish long out of water.
Trout seen fish or dowagers, fan all here.
Grin anew, share flesh of a tortured sole.

Busted

A hot sun for a sweater girl, she fled Reno.
Elegant Florida worse for heat, she runs.
So far we feel heat's on girls around here.
Her far too snug sweater is, of all, her end.

Chased, Unchaste and Chastened	Wine lured her on a soft sofa; the gal errs. No gal fast? Ah, there's word one! Sure, lifer, Refile ruse, no drowser, eh? That's a flagon. Sin's a snare; he fell for her, got wed -- a rout!
Women's Lib	Swollen after eating for hours, dare she? Well, I grunt, she does -- for one hears a fart. The gaffe, or wind, rouses her alert salon. The sworn end's "Hail for a great free soul!"
Words for Fun	Nuts felt for a release, are high on words. English has a lot down for free treasure. Laugh on, feel words are the first reason. Real as life, farers, the word-hunt goes on.
A Peaceful Occupation	Ares' guns, I see, are not for half the world. Words are the neurosis of a gentler half. Ah far-gone role, steal words here -- it's fun! For a felon, these rare wounds are slight.
The Scold	Her tongue has answers for all tired foe. S.O.S.! Harangues all offer the entire word. Oral rage is her loss at the end; we run off. I see none regretful of a harsh last word.
The Put-down	As for the hell of it, ogres wander near us. Then grin a dare: "Those, fellows, are for us!" Wait, for here oglers shun need of altars. La, the offer! We girls err? A thousand noes!
The Sportsperson	Fortunate for her she rides a nag so well. On her round later, she was golf set afire. Sure of all, her great tennis was her food. Final net result was ego; she fed a horror!
The Misogynist	Her leers left anger, sooth of war, unsaid, Rough rations, seen as art, her fellows fed; Hone for gals, fate? How lures err! Instead, Fools rush in where angels fear to tread.

Word Substitution

Perhaps the best-known OuLiPian invention, this literary technique consists of replacing each noun in a text with the seventh noun following it in a prescribed dictionary. Here are several treatments of the last sentence in Wuthering Heights:

Original: I lingered round them, under that benign sky; watched the moths fluttering among the heath and hare-bells; listened to the soft wind breathing through the grass; and wondered how anyone could imagine unquiet slumbers, for the sleepers in that quiet earth.

N + 7, <u>Random House Unabridged</u>: I lingered round them,
under that benign skyflower; watched the Mother Gooses fluttering among the heathenesse and haircots; listened to the
soft windcheater breathing through the grasshopper; and wondered how anyone could imagine unquiet slurs, for the sleeping
chairs in that quiet earthiness.

N + 7, <u>Harrap's Shorter English-French Dictionary</u>: I lingered round them, under that benign skyway; watched the motives
fluttering among the Hebraism and harms; listened to the soft
windmill breathing through the gratuitousness; and wondered
how anyone could imagine unquiet smacks, for the slenderness in
that quiet ease.

W + 10, <u>Harrap's</u> (where W = noun, verb, adjective): I lived
round them, under that bestial slacker, wove the motorcades following among the hecatomb and harlots, lobbed to the sorrowful
windrow brimming through the grave; and wrangled how anyone
could immolate unreceipted slynesses, for the slickers in that
quotable easement.

In the last example, nouns, verbs and adjectives have all been replaced.

In a related experiment, nouns are taken in order from one text,
adjectives from a second and verbs from a third; these are then substituted for the corresponding parts of speech in a fourth text.

LIPOGRAMS

Lipograms are literary texts in which one or more letters have been deliberately suppressed. They represent one of the oldest forms of literary wordplay, with examples dating back to the Greeks. The longest English-language lipogram is a novel, <u>Gadsby</u>, written by Ernest V. Wright without once using the letter E; it was published in 1939.

In very short text passages, it is possible that one or more of the rarer letters of the alphabet will be inadvertently omitted; these accidental events are not ordinarily considered to be lipograms. One can devise a statistical test which will aid in distinguishing between false lipograms and real ones. If k is the expected number of times a given letter should appear in a text (this is ordinarily taken to be the product of the letter's frequency in English and the total number of letters in the text), then the probability of never seeing that letter is equal to $(1/e)^k$, where e is the base of natural logarithms, approximately equal to 2.718. If this probability is sufficiently small (say, less than 0.001), one can conclude with some confidence that the lipogram is real.

Mary Had a Lipogram

Lipogram construction is good training in creative writing, for it forces the student to choose his words carefully. In fact, rewriting a short paragraph or a poem as a lipogram, omitting a different letter each time, is an excellent exercise in learning how to express the same thought in different ways. To demonstrate what can be done, the familiar nursery rhyme by Sarah Josepha Hale, "Mary Had a Little Lamb", has been rewritten five times, omitting its most common letters (S, H, T, E and A) in turn:

> Mary had a little lamb,
> With fleece a pale white hue,
> And everywhere that Mary went
> The lamb kept her in view;
> To academe he went with her,
> Illegal, and quite rare;
> It made the children laugh and play
> To view a lamb in there.
>
> Mary owned a little lamb,
> Its fleece was pale as snow,
> And every place its mistress went
> It certainly would go;
> It followed Mary to class one day

It broke a rigid law;
It made the students giggle aloud,
A lamb in class all saw.

Mary had a pygmy lamb,
His fleece was pale as snow,
And every place where Mary walked
Her lamb did also go;
He came inside her classroom once,
Which broke a rigid rule;
How children all did laugh and play
On seeing a lamb in school.

Mary had a tiny lamb,
Its wool was pallid as snow,
And any spot that Mary did walk
This lamb would always go;
This lamb did follow Mary to school,
Although against a law;
How girls and boys did laugh and play,
That lamb in class all saw.

Polly owned one little sheep,
Its fleece shone white like snow,
Every region where Polly went
The sheep did surely go;
He followed her to school one time,
Which broke the rigid rule;
The children frolicked in their room
To see the sheep in school.

How many letters can one remove from the alphabet before it is impossible to convey a given message accurately? Obviously, there is no hard and fast line; sense, like the Cheshire cat, gradually fades away. The question has considerable relevance to cryptography, because the cryptanalyst will look to letter frequencies for clues in deciphering a message.

To show the possibilities of alphabetic compression, we remove half the letters from the alphabet, using only E, T, A, I, N, S, C, L, D, M, H, R, and P:

Maria had a little sheep,
As pale as rime its hair,
And all the places Maria came
The sheep did tail her there;
In Maria's class it came at last,
A sheep can't enter there;
It made the children clap their hands,
A sheep in class, that's rare.

An even more difficult challenge is to divide the alphabet into two sets of 13 letters apiece, and rewrite the poem twice, using each set

of letters once. For example, one might begin "Mary has a fubsy ram"
and the other "Pollie owned one piddling ewe".

Poems in Praise of English Phonology

Charles F. Hockett, a linguistics professor at Cornell University,
has written a series of poems that can be regarded as phonetic lipograms: each one omits a different set of consonant phonemes in turn.
He uses these to test his students' ability to identify the missing
sounds. After an introductory stanza and a table classifying 24 con-
sonantal sounds, he presents the poems themselves. To make it easy
for non-linguist readers, the omitted consonants have been indicated
at the left of each poem.

A DEPRIVED TALE

(1)

B,P,
D,T,
G,K

I know a lazy sophomore
who never answers one with sass,
although one's nerves he will harass
with ceaseless songs of Elsinore,
lanthanum ore, the life of Thor,
or similar things of now or yore --
he overflows with useless lore.
His usual fare is farfel, or
alfalfa, saffron, sassafras:
his ethos allows him nothing more.
In summer with a roaring snore
(a shallow genre of snoring roar)
he loafs for miles along a shore
of river or of sea. Alas!
he never, never will amass
resources others have use for.

(2)

Z,S,
Zh,Sh,
J,Ch

I want to make it mighty plain:
he can't abide to work at gain --
to work at all would bring him pain.
I ken he'd only try to try
to mount a hillock, not a high
and mighty peak. 'Twould be awry
were he a top goal to attain
by toil bucolic or urbane;
'twould trap yon brain in endocrane
and break an archetype in twain.
Money to him became inane,
impractical -- he'd nought to buy.
Indeed, an indolent, idle guy,
undoubtedly in time he'll die
a pauper, poor like you and I.

(3)

W,M,
V,F,
B,P,
Y,Zh,
Sh,J,
Ch,Ng,
G,K

Last Tuesday he set out to stroll
under a trestle, to stint the toll;
and there he sighted the trestle-troll
dressed in red sandals, a tattered stole,
and little else. This sort o' dress'll
soon daunt any undaunted soul.
He halted. He knew he had to wrestle
the troll to saunter on under the trestle,
or else retreat. A troll in stress'll
not sit idle -- they're hardly sessile.
The satyr stood on a little knoll
and stared a stare so hostile (yet droll)
that the hero decided to turn around dessil
and hunt a hideout, therein to nestle
until the runt'd returned to his hole.

(4)

L,R,
M,N,
Ng

He was kept at his hideout half a week.
Each day, he poked his head out, to peek
to see if the pixie was at the spot
he'd picked to picket those who sought
to bypass the viaduct. He got
toasted feet (the dust was hot),
cuts at head, gashes by cheek
(the pixie had a jagged beak
which got used quick if he chose to seek
to get away). Yet, at the dot
of eight of the sabbath, the pixie said "eek!",
gave his digits a twisted tweak,
so faded away. The boy, half shot,
took his achy body, quite taut,
off the spot at which he'd got caught
back to the city, without a thought,
without a squeak, too weak to speak,
deposited it atop a cot
to doze two days as a potted sot.

(0)

Don't pester me with your complaints
about the pictures my poetry paints --
I've chosen to work within constraints.
The moral of this silly story
isn't to not be sophomory
nor yet to decipher deep allegory,
but just to determine what I've done,
what types of sounds I decided to shun
in each of the stanzas (except this one).

THEME FOR VARIATIONS

(5)

The bees were buzzing merrily
    along the road as I rode in;
the birds were warbling in G
(or maybe I mean B or D)
    and all the woods were yang and yin.

H,F,
P,Th,
S,T,
Sh,Ch,
K

As I rode down the lonely road
    the rain renewed the mud below.
The reeds, the weeds, the woods, the woad
all in a muddle, were a load
    I barely bore. I bore them though.
Renewing vim and vigor then,
    the vinegar was eager. Ang-
-gry words of bees and birds. Then bang!
My rubber gone, my legs again
removed me there beyond the glen.
    And all the woods were yin and yang:
and all the world was young and yen.

Variation One On A Theme For Variations

(6)

H,F,
P,Th,
S,T,
Sh,Ch,
K

A babbling river wandered by a wood.
A burly bull was grazing by the river;
a big bug nibbled on the bovine's liver,
deeming the menu only middling good.

A boy and girl drew nigh along the road,
ignoring woods and river, nibbler, grazer.
The lad was gazing eager on the load
the maiden lugged there under blood-red blazer.

The lazy bull, aroused, arose and ran,
ran ever nearer, breathing gamey air.
The bug abandoned bovóid and began
a-boring in the boy's legs (they were bare).
The bug then rode the boy away, and there
the girl amused the bull with large élan.

The drama done, the bored woods gave a yawn;
the river, unannoyed, meandered on.

Variation Two (Inversion) On A Theme For Variations

(7)

V,B,
Th,Z,
D,Zh,
J,G

Sing a song for fifty cents,
    a pocket stuffed with oats;
sixty pixie elephants
    sporting fancy coats.
When a raucous klaxon toots
    in yon circus tent
elephancy tusks and foots
    relax, all passion spent.

A king sat counting in a house,
    currency or cheques.
A queen went shopping for her spouse:
    turnips, thirteen pecks.
A footman stretched out, tinkering at
    a teensy foreign car,
when on it stepped an elephant
    like practiced circus star.

HIDDEN MESSAGES

The object of cryptology is to hide messages from those not auth-
orized to receive them by means of various transformations on the
letters known only to the sender and the receiver. Many of these are
the same transformations used by logologists: transposals of letters
within a word, substitutions of one letter for another, insertion or
deletion of letters. It is hardly surprising, therefore, to uncover an
area of wordplay that is neither pure logology nor pure cryptology.
One section describes a form of inverse cryptology -- a technique for
making an encrypted message as easy as possible for the recipient to
understand. This is followed by a collection of puzzles with a crypto-
graphic flavor developed by Walter Penney of Greenbelt, Maryland,
and a difficult tricrypt by Dave Silverman originally published in Word
Ways.

A Readable Polyphonic Cipher

A polyphonic substitution cipher is one in which several different
plaintext letters are enciphered into a single cipher letter or symbol.
Perhaps the most simple and well-known example of a polyphonic substitution cipher is the telephone dial, in which the letters ABC are encoded by the number 2, DEF by 3, GHI by 4, JKL by 5, MNO by 6,
PRS by 7, TUV by 8, and WXY by 9. This is quite different from the
well-known (monophonic) substitution cipher, in which each plaintext
letter is associated with a different cipher letter -- if A is encoded by
T, then no other letter of the alphabet is also encoded by T. (However,
the opposite of the polyphonic substitution cipher is the homophonic
substitution cipher, in which a single plaintext letter can be enciphered
into several different cipher letters or symbols -- for example, E
might be represented by the number-pairs 13, 28 or 94.)

Superficially, polyphonic substitution ciphers resemble lipograms.
In both cases, the reader is confronted with a message which contains
fewer different letters (or symbols) than the normal 26-letter alphabet. However, a lipogram is restricted to those words which contain
the allowable letters, whereas a polyphonic cipher allows any word to
be encoded. In lipograms, all the words look normal but thoughts
must be expressed in a circuitous way; in polyphonic ciphers, the
thoughts are normal enough but many words are spelled in weird ways.

Polyphonic substitution ciphers have been known for more than
three centuries; David Kahn's The Codebreakers (MacMillan, 1967)
states that the Argentis, a family of cryptologists employed by the

Pope shortly before 1600, used a polyphonic cipher. However, these ciphers seem to have remained outside the mainstream of cryptologic activity, probably because of their inherent ambiguity. If a cipher letter can represent several different plaintext letters, it is quite likely that two different plaintext words will lead to the same cipher equivalent. In the August 1970 Word Ways, Dave Silverman pointed out that the telephone dial encodes both PYGMIES and SWINGER in the same way: 7946437. The article "Word-Pairs Differing in a Single Letter" in the May 1969 Word Ways demonstrated that no polyphonic cipher is entirely free of possible single-word ambiguities.

Should then such ciphers be discarded as unworkable? Not necessarily, because single-word ambiguities ought to be resolvable by looking at the context -- other words on either side. It is the purpose of this article to demonstrate that a careful selection of the way in which letters are encoded should hold the ambiguity to a minimum.

How much compression can be allowed in a polyphonic substitution cipher before the output becomes unreadable? Clearly, a cipher allowing 15 or more different symbols ought to cause little trouble; the 11 rarest English letters occur only about ten per cent of the time in normal text. On the other hand, any cipher which jams the entire alphabet into only 5 different symbols is bound to sound like an idiot mumbling Sanskrit in his sleep. Since the ten digits form a natural encoding (as in the telephone dial), it is reasonable to ask whether or not one can construct a polyphonic cipher on this base. Let us make the task a bit harder by insisting that one of the ten digits (say, 0) must be reserved exclusively as an indicator of word spacing, leaving only nine digits to carry the weight of 26 letters.

To make a long story short, we propose that the following polyphonic substitution cipher is about as good as any that can be devised to produce readable text from the cipher output:

1 E	4 I, L, B	7 R, Y, W
2 T, X, Z	5 O, G, J	8 S, F, M 0 Space
3 A, C, Q	6 N, P, K, V	9 H, D, U

Letters have been allocated to digits by a trial-and-error procedure attempting to satisfy various objectives which will become apparent presently.

Suppose that a message is written in this cipher; how does one decode it? Perhaps the simplest technique is to place the alternative letters in a vertical column with the commonest letter at the bottom, and look for patterns of letters that form words. For example:

```
  V                    VV V
BK MUJWZ B QM QJ KKBKQ  U BJ ZU BW MQBZU
LP FDGYX L CF CGPPLPC  D LGXD LY FCLXD
IN SHORT I AS AONNINAEH IOTH IR SAITH....
```

Reading along the bottom, the words IN SHORT I leap out at once. AS does not seem too likely a follow-on to I, but we note that AM is a legal alternative. The next word is obviously a verb, but the bottom line is gibberish, and the next three words are none too clear either. (Before reading on, the reader is encouraged to try and figure out what these words are.) Is it possible that we have been too ambitious in restricting ourself to a nine-symbol code?

What is needed is a way to present to the reader the most plausible possibilities for the hidden words. One way to do this is to ask the following question: given two successive symbols, what is the most plausible bigram of letters corresponding to these symbols? For example, in the fourth word in the message above, AO is clearly a very unlikely bigram (AORTA and GAOL come to mind), and in fact the bigram CO is overwhelmingly more plausible (AG is a second choice). If the excess verbiage could be pruned out and CO exhibited as a first choice, the message ought to be much easier to read.

This, in fact, is the primary basis upon which the alphabet was allocated to digits. Fletcher Pratt's <u>Secret and Urgent</u> (Blue Ribbon Books, 1942) gives in Table VIII of the Appendix a list of the 70 commonest bigrams occuring in English text, and in Table V the frequency of occurrence of letters as initials and terminals in English words. Each entry in the table below is the commonest bigram (according to Fletcher Pratt) corresponding to a digit at the left followed by a digit at the top; for example, if the pair 72 is encountered, the table suggests that RT is the most likely plaintext bigram corresponding to this cipher. 57 of the 81 bigrams in the table are included among the 70 commonest bigrams in the English language; in fact, the 30 commonest bigrams are all included in the table (DE is the first one that does not appear).

		0	1	2	3	4	5	6	7	8	9
Space	0	-	-	- E	- T	- A	- I	- O	- P	- W	- S	- H
E	1	E-	EE	ET	EA	EL	EG	EN	ER	ES	ED
TXZ	2	T-	TE	TT	TA	TI	TO	XP	TR	TS	TH
ACQ	3	A-	CE	AT	CA	AL	CO	AN	AR	AS	CH
ILB	4	L-	LE	IT	IC	LI	IO	IN	LY	IS	LD
OGJ	5	O-	GE	OT	OA	OL	OO	ON	OR	OF	OU
NPKV	6	N-	NE	NT	NC	NI	NG	NN	PR	NS	ND
RYW	7	Y-	RE	RT	RA	RI	RO	RN	RR	RS	RD
SFM	8	S-	SE	ST	MA	S I	SO	MP	FR	SS	SH
HDU	9	D-	HE	UT	HA	HI	DO	UN	UR	US	DU

How is this table used to decode a cipher? Note that the terminal letter of one recommended bigram may not coincide with the initial letter of the next recommended bigram; for example, 72 leads to RT but 26 to XP. To get around this problem, the putative plaintext is written on two lines, with a shift from one line to the other whenever there is a disagreement of this sort. Returning to the earlier message, how does it now look?

```
IN SH     L AS A            D I   MAL D AND ETNERI
     DORT I    CONNINCED IOTH LY S  ITH        XP  LENCE


     G S  INTAL          IS ON THIS EARTH    NG
THAT TO MAL     IN ONES SEL                D IS POT A


     USHIN IUT A PASTISE IS W   RIL I LINE SIS NI
HARD       LD    NC         RE WLI L I        MPLY


     RISELY.
AND W
```

When this "translation" was tried out on the author's wife and
teen-aged daughter, both were rather quickly able to figure out most
of the words from the context; the eighth word (actually, FAITH)
was the only one to cause real trouble. The original message, taken
from Thoreau's Walden, is:

In short, I am convinced, both by faith and experience, that to
maintain one's self on this earth is not a hardship but a pastime,
if we will live simply and wisely.

Of the 128 letters in this message, the commonest-bigram scheme
identified all but 11 to within at most two possible alternatives; even
one really rare letter, X, was spotted.

The reader may want to try his hand at decoding another message
with the aid of the commonest-bigram table:

```
42048 06520 61318 83770 29320 30836 08959 49013 76094
80446 46504 70291 08713 20580 94804 75709 64188 09108
71328 01384 17029 36040 95
```

The message has been divided into groups of five for ease in reading.
The answer can be found at the end of this chapter.

So far, we have talked about ways to make a polyphonic substitution
cipher as easy as possible to read. Usually the objective of a cipher is
just the opposite. Can this cipher be used for secret communications?
Suppose that the assignment of letters to digits was rearranged in a
way known only to the sender and the recipient; for example, BLI
might be encoded as 7, QCA as 2, a space as 5, and so forth. (The
shuffling of digits could be easily remembered by means of a ten-letter isogram, such as BACKGROUND or COMPUTABLE.) To improve the security of such a cipher system, a secondary objective
in assigning letters to digits was to equalize the frequency with which
the different digits would appear in normal English text. Although
perfect balance could not be achieved, the range of variation is small:
among the digits 1 through 9, the digit 1 will appear most frequently
(about 13 per cent of the time), while the digits 5 and 6 will appear
least often (about 10 per cent of the time each). Unfortunately, the

security of the cipher is seriously compromised by the fact that
spaces appear much more often -- perhaps 20 per cent of the time in
normal English text. The would-be cryptanalyst can easily identify
which digit is being used to represent a space, and it is then an easy
matter to recover the digits corresponding to A and I, the only two
single-letter words. Anyone contemplating using this cipher, therefore, is strongly encouraged to omit all spaces between words, even
though this makes recovery of the plaintext more difficult.

Penney Puzzles (Walter Penney)

Puzzle 1

    An automatic card shuffler always rearranges the cards in the
same way if the setting is the same. A set of twelve cards bearing
the letters G O L D E N B I N A R Y is put through the machine, and
the cards, in the order in which they emerge, are put through the
machine a second time. They come out A N I N O Y G R E D B L.
What message did the cards convey after the first operation, assuming the setting is left unchanged for the second operation?

Puzzle 2

    The letters of the alphabet are converted into their International
Morse Code equivalents, with a space between each pair of letters
and two spaces between each pair of words. Each pair of elements
(for example, dot-space, dash-dash and so on) is then assigned a
number from 1 to 9 (for example, 5 may correspond to dash-dot,
and 3 to space-dash). A message written in this system becomes:
5 1 2 5 3 7 4 2 9 3 2 2 8 2 3 1 4 6 3 7 3 7 3 2 5 7 4 2 3 4 6 4 2 8 1 4 7.
What pair of elements corresponds to each number, and what does
the message say?

    For convenience, the International Morse Code is given below:

A dot dash	J dot dash dash dash	S dot dot dot
B dash dot dot dot	K dash dot dash	T dash
C dash dot dash dot	L dot dash dot dot	U dot dot dash
D dash dot dot	M dash dash	V dot dot dot dash
E dot	N dash dot	W dot dash dash
F dot dot dash dot	O dash dash dash	X dash dot dot dash
G dash dash dot	P dot dash dash dot	Y dash dot dash dash
H dot dot dot dot	Q dash dash dot dash	Z dash dash dot dot
I dot dot	R dot dash dot	

Puzzle 3

Sixteen letters are written in a four-by-four square with rows
and columns labeled 1 through 4. Thus, a letter in the second row
and the third column can be converted into the pair of numbers 2 3.
The word LUMBERJACK is converted into a series of numbers
using these co-ordinates, and the number 1 is added at the beginning
of this series and the number 4 at the end of this series. This new
series of twenty-two numbers is broken up into pairs, and recon-
verted into letters using the same four-by-four square; the result is
B E S O L K H C U A I.   Another word is similarly treated, using
the same square, but with a 4 added at the beginning and a 1 at the
end. This comes out T M O C H R B N S S E. What is the original
word?

Puzzle 4

The words of a saying are written one below the other, lined up
on the left. The initial letters are then taken off, followed by the
second letters, etc., blanks being skipped. For example, 'Roses
are red violets are blue' becomes by this process R A R V A
B O R E I   R L S E D   O E U E L   E S E T S. Read the following:
T I N F L   A B T B U   W A H S O   R I O O E   S O W E I
K O A R A   R G E K R   L Y E A D   T S E.

Puzzle 5

A certain quotation containing 26 letters is written below a normal alphabet and used for the cipher equivalents of a simple substitution system. (Note that a cipher letter may stand for more than
one plain letter with this scheme.) These equivalents are then used
to encipher the quotation. For example, 'Give me liberty or give
me death' becomes:

A B C D E F G H I J K L M N O P Q R S T U V W X Y Z
G I V E M E L I B E R T Y O R G I V E M E D E A T H
L B D M Y M T B I M V M T R V L B D M Y M E M G M I

What message is given by Y I Y V N E A S L R O E E E E U A I Y
V A U A U A L?

Puzzle 6

For haggling purposes a curio dealer enciphered the cost prices
on his tags, replacing each digit by a letter. To improve his bar-

gaining position, a shrewd customer noted the letters on the tags of three items, and at various times casually asked the price of each. The tags read NL. MI, CR. IK and AP. EI, and the prices asked were respectively $39.69, $53.46 and $87.75. The customer correctly assumed that these all represented the same percentage mark-up. What did these items cost?

Puzzle 7

The word ALUMINUM has the pattern 12345634 since the third letter is the same as the seventh letter, and the fourth is the same as the last, the others being all different. The word MOLECULE has the same pattern. Put them together and you get an ALUMINUM MOLECULE. Try to solve the pattern pairs below, aided by the clues.

1. 1 2 2 3 4 5 3 6   Wrongdoer taken into custody.
2. 1 2 3 1 4 5 3 6   Lady flier who cannot tell a lie.
3. 1 2 3 2 1 4 5 6   Monster threatening evil.
4. 1 2 3 2 4 2 5 6   Something denied to the military.
5. 1 2 3 2 4 5 6 3   Tourists in native costumes.
6. 1 2 3 3 4 5 3 6   Fighters easily taken in.
7. 1 2 3 4 3 5 1 6   Unexpected pardon.
8. 1 2 3 4 5 1 2 6   Shoulder bone that has been repaired.
9. 1 2 3 4 5 3 1 6   Minor battle along the shore
10. 1 2 3 4 5 3 4 6   Portrait in oils done with skill and taste.
11. 1 2 3 4 5 4 2 6   Witty prestidigitator.
12. 1 2 3 4 5 6 2 1   Disadvantaged scholars.
13. 1 2 3 4 5 6 2 3   Signals given in bull-fighting.
14. 1 2 3 4 5 6 3 1   Signs that might make diagnosis difficult.
15. 1 2 3 4 5 6 5 3   Nurseryman afflicted with rickets.

ANSWERS

A Readable Polyphonic Cipher

It is not necessary that a man should earn his living by the sweat of his brow unless he sweats easier than I do. Thoreau, Walden.

Penney Puzzles

Puzzle 1: If we number the letters of G O L D E N B I N A R Y from 1 through 12, we see that the final arrangement is either 10 6 8 9 2 12 1 11 5 4 7 3 or 10 9 8 6 2 12 1 11 5 4 7 3, depending upon the positions of the two N's. The intermediate arrangement can be easily

deduced with a little trial and error. For example, assume that the
first number is 2; then the second number must be 10 in order to en-
sure that two successive operations convert 1 into 10. Eventually
one discovers that the second permutation given above is the result
of two applications of the permutation 3 5 10 11 9 7 12 4 2 8 6 1, which
yields the message L E A R N B Y D O I N G.

Puzzle 2: If we make all possible assumptions for 2 and 8 and form
the fragment 2 2 8 2, eliminating all assumptions leading to three
spaces in a row, five or more dots and dashes in a row with no
space, or an impossible combination (dot dot dash dash, dot dash
dot dash, dash dash dash dot, dash dash dash dash), we are left
with a small number of possibilities. Extending these to the fragment 3 2 2 8 2 3 by making all admissible assumptions for 3, again
eliminating the impossible sequences, and continuing with 9 and 1,
we are soon able to eliminate everything except WELL BEGUN IS
HALF DONE.

Puzzle 3: From the data we see that B, K and U are in the first
row of the square, and A, E and O in the first column. Likewise, T
is in the fourth row and I in the fourth column. Also, C and S are in
the same row as the column containing J and U. Proceeding in this
way and using all the information about the rows and columns containing the other letters, we are able to construct a number of squares
containing 15 letters which satisfy all the conditions. The sixteenth
letter must be the missing W.

However, only the two squares   O B K U   O K B U
shown to the right permit a word   E L N J   A R H I
to be constructed from TMOCHR-   A H R I   E N L J
BNSSE, namely, JOURNALIST.   M T C S   M C T S

Puzzle 4: The initial T is most likely to be followed by H. If we
line up the H in position 13, we get good letter pairs until the end
when we come across WW. Although there are words with two consecutive W's (GLOWWORM, for example), this combination seems unlikely. It is more probable that we have passed a one-letter word
which would throw off the spacing. Skipping a space for A (the only
candidate) and continuing with the third column we get, with a little
juggling because of short words, THERE IS NO FRIGATE LIKE A
BOOK TO BEAR US WORLDS AWAY.

Puzzle 5: Note that B in the original alphabet translates to I in the
message, I in the original alphabet translates to L in the message,
and so on, forming a chain. The longest such chain is J R I L E N.
Let us assume in turn J = A, B, ... , Z and trace through the let-

ters so determined, until an inconsistency develops.   We find the only consistent sequences are E . . R Y . . . U D . A . A . . . V . . L I . . N . and E . . . Y . . . U T . A . A . . . V . R L I . . N . Continuing in this way we find the second letter is P, V or X, the third letter is E, etc.   We soon learn that EVERY CLOUD HAS A SILVER LINING.

Puzzle 6:   The original prices were $ 36. 75, $ 49. 50 and $ 81. 25, representing a markup of 8 per cent.   The system of letter equivalents is seen to be based on the words PENCIL MARK.

Puzzle 7:   1. arrested offender   2. truthful aviatrix   3. sinister werewolf   4. civilian monopoly   5. colorful visitors   6. gullible warriors   7. surprise clemency   8. restored clavicle   9. seacoast skirmish   10. artistic painting   11. humorous magician   12. deprived students   13. toreador gestures   14. spurious symptoms   15. rachitic gardener.

WORD NETWORKS

Most logologists have noticed that some words, such as SHAME and SHARE, are relatively near each other, whereas others, such as TONIC and WATER, are far apart. If pressed for a definition of the distance between two words, they might suggest that it is equal to the number of letters that must be altered to transmute one word into the other. The nearer two words are to each other, the easier it is to accidentally change one into another by a typographical miscue. A large number of English words are only one letter apart, a situation humorously exploited for many years in the Readers Digest column "Pardon, Your Slip Is Showing". Students of the language have suggested that English has more potentiality for mistakes of this sort than other languages do; see, for example, Petr Beckmann's The Structure of Language: A New Approach (Golem Press, 1972) for the development of this idea.

The object of this article is to investigate the nearness of short words in a systematic fashion. Imagine, for example, all three-letter words written down on a sheet of paper, with lines joining every pair of words that differs in only one letter, such as ERA and BRA, or BAT and BUT, or SEE and SEA. One can ask many questions about the properties of this word network -- for example, what word has the largest number of lines emanating from it? are all words in a single network, or are there several networks isolated from each other, like an archipelago?

The answers to these questions depend, of course, on the number of words one includes in the study. The difficulties of characterizing word networks are in general so great that it has been necessary to severely restrict the vocabulary. In particular, we use only those words that appear in boldface type in the main section (pp. 1-592) of the Merriam-Webster Pocket Dictionary. Hyphenated words, suffixes, prefixes and abbreviations are omitted, as are words listed without further definition (anti-, in-, over-, re-, self-, sub-, super- and un-). Even so, the vocabulary size is so large that it is feasible to show actual networks only for two-letter words and (in part) three-letter words in the first part of this article. The vocabulary sizes for various word-lengths are given below:

```
2-letter words:  38   4-letter words: 1843   7-letter words: 4591
3-letter words: 541   5-letter words: 2798   8-letter words: 4415
                      6-letter words: 4056
```

The task of searching for words near other words was greatly
facilitated by a positional word list, Volume 1 of the Word Builder's
Handbook, published in 1972 by Computer Puzzle Library, Fort
Worth, Texas, covering words from 2 to 8 letters in length. (A companion volume covers words from 9 to 15 letters in length.) The
claim is made that these volumes were prepared with meticulous
care using modern computer capabilities to provide the greatest
possible accuracy, and indeed the accuracy is greater than in other
publications of this type. Computer processing insures that the
various rearranged lists all contain the same words with none accidentally left out, but it does not guard against keypunch errors in
preparing the original list. Two such keypunch errors: EUREKA
is spelled UEREKA, and YCLEPT is spelled YCELPT.

In this article (the first of two parts) we study three different word networks, consisting of words from two to four letters
in length. Broadly speaking, most of the shorter words of a given
length are joined in a single network, whereas the longer words of a
given length are scattered among a number of independent networks.
It is for this reason that word ladders (chains of the form LESS-
LOSS-LOSE-LORE-MORE) are usually restricted to words of five
or fewer letters. The chance is quite small that a random pair of
seven-letter or eight-letter words can be joined by a word ladder in
the Pocket Dictionary.

Two-Letter Word Network

As there are only 38 two-letter words in the Pocket Dictionary,
it is an easy matter to map the entire network. In the diagram on the
next page, a group of three or more words differing only in their final
letter is listed in a row and joined by solid lines; similarly, a group
of three or more words differing only in their first letter is listed in
a column and joined by solid lines. Solid lines act as a kind of shorthand for the considerably more numerous lines that should be plotted
between every pair of words in a group; for example, the fact that
one can move from OR to OF by means of parallel solid lines should
be interpreted as meaning that one can move from OR to OF in a single step, leapfrogging OK, OX and ON. Groups of only two words
are joined by dotted lines.

The most important feature of this network is that no two-letter
words are left out. Note, however, that a slightly different vocabulary would have broken it into two independent networks -- all that is
necessary is to remove GO, or GI, or PI, or PA, or MA.

It is useful to introduce here several properties of a word network
that are helpful in visualizing larger networks that cannot be so easily
diagrammed. What word in the network has the maximal ambiguity --
that is, what word can be transmuted into the largest number of other
words with the change of only one letter? AN can be transmuted into

the eight words IN, ON, AY, AX, AM, AD, AT and AS; similarly,
AS and AY have eight near neighbors.

The densest part of the network can be identified not by a single
word but by a group of words in a rectangular array, such as OX-AX-
ON-AN. Such patterns have previously been called garble groups in

```
or——ok——ox—— on——of                    us---up
          |      |      |                      |
          |     in——if——id——it——is
          |      |      |      |      |      |
         ay——ax——an——am——ad——at——as
          |
be---by                    to——tv——tb
 |    |                      |
me——my——ma                  no
 |      |                    |
he     pa---pi              do
 |       |                   |
ye      gi----go            go
 |                           |
we                          lo
                             |
                            so
```

Word Ways; in response to a query, Leslie Card exhibited various
maximum-size garble groups in the November 1970 and February
1971 issues. In the above network, it is easy to locate the largest
garble group: IN-AN-ID-AD-IT-AT-IS-AS. Since the first letter
can take on either of two values and the second letter can take on
any of four values, a shorthand notation for the shape of the garble
group is given by (24). Note that the maximum garble group includes two of the three maximally ambiguous words.

A slightly more sophisticated concept is the span of a word network. For any two words in a network, there is a shortest path
joining them -- for example, the shortest path between MA and AX
is MA-my-ay-AX with three steps, although the five-step path MA-
me-be-by-ay-AX is also possible. As the initial and final words
are varied, how long can such a shortest path be? Examining the
network, it is not hard to see that the shortest path joining UP to
TB has eleven steps: UP-us-as-ay-my-ma-pa-pi-gi-go-to-TB.
A similar number of steps is required to join UP to TV, OR to
TV or TB, OF to TB or TV, and OK to TV or TB. Thus, the span
of this word network is eleven.

There are (26)(26) = 676 possible ways that words of two letters can be formed. The word network of 38 words occupies less
than six per cent of this space. How widely scattered through the
space are the words in the network? One measure of scatter was
introduced by Dmitri Borgmann in "Irrelevance" in Beyond Language (Scribner's, 1967). How many words can be found in the

network with the property that all the first letters of the words are
different from each other and all the second letters of the words are
also different from each other? Put another way, how many words
can be found which have a maximum resistance to ambiguity with
each other? A little experimentation reveals that there are several
different ways that ten such words can be selected; one such set is
TV, NO, GI, PA, MY, HE, AX, OK, IN and US.

Three-Letter Word Networks

The three-letter word network is considerably more complicated
than the two-letter one. To begin with, there is no single network
which includes all 541 three-letter words; the twelve words listed below are isolated from the main network and from each other:

ebb	gnu	ism	nth	ohm	urn
emu	imp	its	obi	ova	use

In the February 1969 Word Ways, Rudolph Castown proposed the
term singularity for a word which does not connect with any other
word, and the term isolano for a group of words which do not connect with the main word network (i.e., the largest network). Later,
Dave Silverman used isolano for a single isolated word, and ignored
the problem of naming an isolated group. We shall adopt the latter
nomenclature, and note that there are twelve three-letter isolanos
in the Pocket Dictionary.

The remaining 529 words form a single network which is far too
complicated to diagram. To give some flavor of the network, we
have diagrammed on the next page those 86 words which begin with
the vowels A, E, I and O (there are no words beginning with U other
than the two isolanos above), the sparsest section of the network.
Note that the network is now three-dimensional -- a group of words
differing only in the third letter is listed in a row, a group of words
differing only in the second letter, in a column, and a group of
words differing only in the first letter, along a diagonal meant to
suggest a vertical to the page. It may be helpful to think of the network as the somewhat incomplete steel framework of a building with
four floors -- words beginning with I in the basement, then words
beginning with O, next words beginning with A, and finally words
beginning with E on the roof.

The fifteen underlined words near the top of the diagram are the
only places where this part of the network connects with words beginning with consonants. Already, this hints at a property that will become more pronounced in later networks -- it is relatively difficult
to cross over from words beginning with vowels to words beginning
with consonants, and words beginning with vowels are far more likely
to form isolanos or isolated groups.

To get some idea of the undiagrammed dense part of the network,
let us consider the various properties introduced earlier. The net-

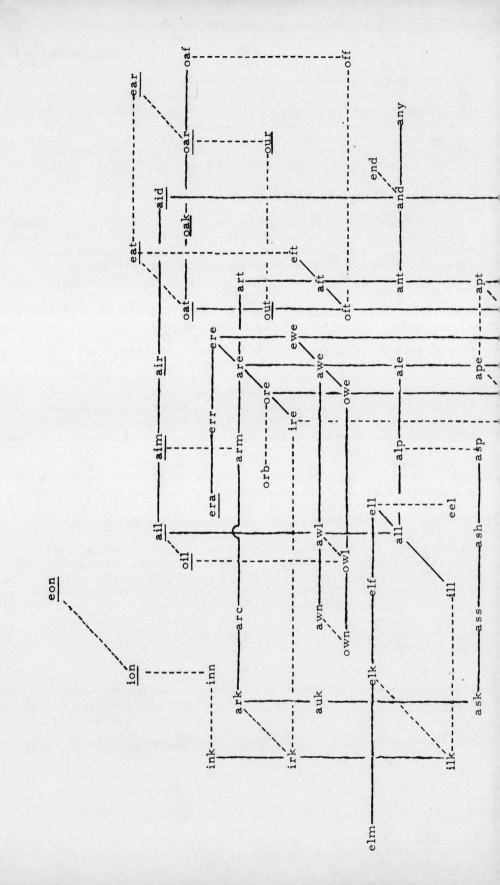

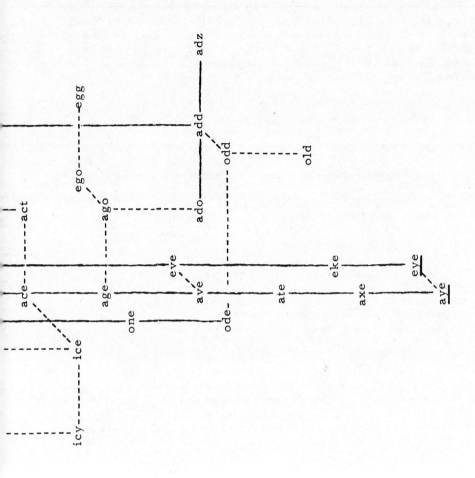

work word having maximal ambiguity is almost certainly SAY with
25 lines joining it: SAC, SAD, SAG, SAP, SAT, SAW, SHY, SKY,
SLY, SOY, SPY, STY, BAY, CAY, DAY, FAY, GAY, HAY, JAY,
LAY, MAY, NAY, PAY, RAY and WAY. (In the diagrammed part,
one can easily check that the most ambiguous word is ARE with 16
connections.)

This network is exceptionally rich in large garble groups. The
largest one is believed to be the (523) group given below:

cap	cop	hap	hop	map	mop	sap	sop	tap	top
cat	cot	hat	hot	mat	mot	sat	sot	tat	tot
caw	cow	haw	how	maw	mow	saw	sow	taw	tow

The second and third best garble groups are given below; their
shapes are (515) and (432), respectively. Note that the (515)
group fails to exploit one of the available dimensions; all of its
words have A as their second letter:

cad	cap	cat	caw	cay		hat	pat	sat	tat
had	hap	hat	haw	hay		hit	pit	sit	tit
mad	map	mat	maw	may		hot	pot	sot	tot
pad	pap	pat	paw	pay					
sad	sap	sat	saw	say		hap	pap	sap	tap
						hip	pip	sip	tip
						hop	pop	sop	top

Note that HAP, HAT, SAP and SAT occur in all three groups, suggesting the general area of the densest part of the network. (There
are no three-dimensional garble groups in the diagrammed part, although there are numerous two-dimensional groups of sizes 4 and 6,
and one of size 8.)

The span of this word network is somewhat difficult to determine.
It is conjectured that no word-pairs exist having a greater minimum
path-length than IVY and YOU: IVY-icy-ice-ire-are-arm-aim-dim-
din-win-won-yon-YOU is one of several equivalent twelve-step paths.
Notice that the span is barely greater than that of the two-word network, although the vocabulary size is more than ten times as large.
Clearly, it is a much more densely connected network than the earlier one was.

The number of words having maximum resistance to ambiguity
rises from ten to seventeen: one such list is ADD, BRA, CAR,
DEW, EBB, FLY, GNU, HIT, IMP, JOG, NTH, OWL, PYX, RUN,
SKI, USE and WHO. Word lists of this type are apt to make dispro-
portionate use of isolanos; five of the twelve are represented here.
The theoretical maximum number of such words is 26, so that this
list is quite a respectable one.

Four-Letter Word Networks

Only 2.2 per cent of all three-letter words in the Pocket Dictionary are isolated from the main network; this percentage rises to
10.5 when four-letter words are considered. The isolanos begin to
have an interesting group structure of their own; for example, one
group of eleven words is unconnected to the main network. A listing of all isolano groups follows:

adze	apex	doff	huge	kyat	nuts	ovum	upon
agog	apse	drys	hymn	liar	obey	raja	urdu
ague	arch	echo	ibex	lira	oboe	ruby	urge
ahoy	ashy	egis	iced	luau	odds	stye	uric
alga	auld	envy	iffy	lynx	odor	suds	user
alms	aura	epee	inky	magi	okay	sync	veto
amok	avow	epic	iota	memo	okra	tabu	whom
ammo	awol	espy	jehu	meow	once	taxi	whys
anal	bias	evil	judo	myna	onyx	thou	xmas
ankh	crux	gaff	kayo	nazi	orgy	tyro	zebu
	dais	hobo	khan	nova	ours	ugly	

```
afar-ajar      army-arty      edam-exam      mama-maya
amah-ayah      axes-axis      ibis-iris      ogle-ogre
ante-anti      does-goes      idol-idyl      oleo-olio


anus-onus      anew-knew      also-alto
     opus           knee           auto      icon-ikon-iron


bevy-levy      idly-idle      eddy-edgy      opal-oral-oval
     leva           isle           edge
                                             quad-quai-quay
               dodo-dido
                    lido


aged
abed-abet      into-onto-unto      ache-acme-acne-acre
     abut               undo


each-etch              nigh                  ally
     itch-inch         high                  ably
          inca    sikh-sigh       abbe-able
huff                        sign             axle
ruff
luff   tiff            edit                  oxen
muff-miff              exit                  open
puff             omit-emit        eden  omen-amen
cuff             obit     emir    even-oven
buff                                         ever-over-aver
                                             ewer
```

The isolation of words beginning with vowels is quite marked. All
but 46 of the 171 vowel words are in the isolano groups above, and the
rest are connected to the main network only in small clusters.

All clusters involving more than two words are diagrammed below.

```
          WIRY                          area-urea
          airy              GRID-arid-aria
ZERO-aero-aery-eery-VERY    acid
          awry              amid
          away              avid        VASE-ease-else
          SWAY                                easy
                                        VAST-east-erst
```

STEM-item-idem-idea-ides

However, that part of the network consisting of words beginning with consonants appears to be fairly strongly connected. Most of these words are of the form CVCC, CVVC or CVCV (where C stands for a consonant and V a vowel); there are many bridges between each pair of these patterns.

The network word having maximal ambiguity is probably WARE, which has 24 lines joining it: BARE, CARE, DARE, FARE, HARE, MARE, PARE, RARE, TARE, WERE, WIRE, WORE, WADE, WAGE, WAKE, WALE, WANE, WAVE, WARD, WARM, WARN, WARP, WART and WARY.

Four-letter garble groups are markedly smaller than three-letter ones, suggesting that the densest part of the four-letter network is somewhat more open than the densest part of the three-letter network. Two sixteen-word garble groups are known, with shapes of (4221) and (4141):

```
dane  fane  mane  wane      bale  bane  bare  bate
dine  fine  mine  wine      dale  dane  dare  date
                            male  mane  mare  mate
dare  fare  mare  ware      pale  pane  pare  pate
dire  fire  mire  wire
```

Note that neither of these garble groups has a pattern in which there are changes of all letters. In geometric terms, there is no garble group from the Pocket Dictionary that exploits all four dimensions. Although garble groups with the shape (2222) are possible (see Castown's article on word ladders in the August 1968 issue), words not in the Pocket Dictionary must be used. The nearest approach using Pocket Dictionary words appears to be:

```
bard band   bare bane    ward wand    ware wane
---- bond   bore bone    word ----    wore ----
```

The number of words having maximum resistance to ambiguity remains at the high level of seventeen: AMMO, CZAR, ETCH, FIZZ, HUSK, IKON, KNEW, LYNX, NEWT, OGLE, PLUM, RAJA, TWIG, URDU, WHYS, SPRY and YOGI. One should note that only eight of these words come from the main network.

TRANSPOSALS

A transposal of a word is a rearrangement of its letters into a new word, as CORSET to ESCORT or AGNOSTIC to COASTING. Although the words transposal and anagram are often used interchangeably, this practice is to be deplored. An anagram is a transposal of a word or phrase into another word or phrase which has the same meaning, as ENDEARMENT to TENDER NAME or H. M. S. PINAFORE to NAME FOR SHIP. Anagramming has been practiced for centuries, but transposing has been recognized as a separate art for only the past half-century or so. Although long transposals were published a century ago (the fine ENUMERATION - MOUNTAINEER appeared in the Saturday Evening Post in 1879), transposals are not discussed at all in A Key to Puzzledom, a handbook of wordplay compiled in 1906 by members of The Eastern Puzzlers' League.

Long Well-Mixed Transposals

By the middle of the 1920s, however, the transposal enjoyed a considerable popularity. Three major articles on transposals appear in the National Puzzlers' League's Enigma of that time (October 1924, December 1924, June 1925). The leading constructor then was Hercules B. McPherrin of Denver, Colorado (1874 - 1953), the first person to discover a considerable number of really long transposals. The first book devoted to transposals, the Nuttall Dictionary of Anagrams, was compiled by A. R. Ball and published by Frederick Warne & Co. in 1937. Apparently Ball did not have access to the National Puzzlers' League work in this field, for the longest transposal in his book is CERTIFICATION - RECTIFICATION, a relatively trivial one.

It was early recognized that very long transposals are more likely than not to consist of interchanges of only two or three letters, as CONVERSATION to CONSERVATION, or of large segments of the word, as HYDROPNEUMOPERICARDIUM to PNEUMOHYDROPERI-CARDIUM or CHOLECYSTODUODENOSTOMY to DUODENOCHOLECY-STOSTOMY. (At 22 letters apiece, these are the longest transposals for which both words appear in boldface in Webster's Second.) Much more interesting to the logologist are transposals in which the letters of one word are well-mixed in the second one.

To fix ideas, this article introduces the following definition of well-mixed: a transposal in which no more than three consecutive letters of one word appear as three consecutive letters in the other. For example, consider the transposal NONGEOMETRICAL - INCONGLOMERATE

authored by Murray Pearce in the November 1974 Enigma.   The trigrams ONG and OME appear in both words, but there are no other trigram or bigram matches.   The quality of this transposal can be succinctly characterized by the number sequence (2,0), denoting the number of trigrams in common followed by the number of bigrams in common.   It is possible to find perfectly-mixed transposals in which no
bigrams or trigrams in one word are repeated in the other; for example, Murray Pearce's NITROMAGNESITE - REGIMENTATIONS, appearing in the August 1971 Enigma, has this property.

This article lists all known well-mixed transposals of 13 or more
letters, giving credit, where known, to the earliest appearance of the
transposal.   The first of these to be discovered was found by accident.
In the September 15, 1906 issue of The Ardmore Puzzler, "Rusticus"
posed the anagram IS A REVERTING TO, intending that the answer be
TERGIVERSATION.   However, "The Poser" came up with the alternative solution INTERROGATIVES.   Subsequently, "Alec Sander",
an Ardmore assistant editor, sent the pair as a transposal puzzle to
the Newark Evening News.

This stood as a record-length well-mixed transposal for nearly
twenty years, until Hercules McPherrin proposed the 15-letter pair
DECHLORINATIONS - ORNITHOSCELIDAN in the June 1925 Enigma.
The first word is an inferred plural of a boldface word in Webster's
Second; the second word also appears in boldface in this source.   He
followed this up in the December 1927 issue with the equally remarkable CINEMATOGRAPHER - MEGACHIROPTERAN.

These in turn stood as record-length well-mixed transposals for
almost 50 years, until Charles E. Holding of Silver Spring, Maryland
published the 17-letter BASIPARACHROMATIN - MARSIPOBRANCHI-
ATA in the October 1971 Enigma.   Notice that these words share one
trigram (SIP) and five bigrams (AR, RA, CH, MA and AT), and
hence the transposal quality is (1,5); nevertheless, even the most
exacting logologist would grant that it is a well-mixed transposal.

The search for transposals is a task ideally suited for a high-speed
digital computer.   As part of a research project to ascertain the lexi-
cal capabilities of the computer, Dennis Ritchie, a member of techni-
cal staff of Bell Telephone Laboratories, sorted out the boldface words
of Webster's Unabridged (Second Edition) into a transposal dictionary
in 1973.   In addition, he programmed the computer to construct derived forms of words in boldface in Webster's Collegiate (Seventh
Edition), adding these words to the stockpile available for transposal.
Letting V stand for a vowel and C for a consonant, his rules for word-
formation can be summarized as follows:

1) Gerunds: if verb ends in Vc, add -king; if verb ends in CVC
   with last syllable stressed and final letter not x or w, double
   the final consonant and add -ing; if verb ends in Ce, drop the
   e before adding -ing.
2) Past tenses: if verb ends in e, add -d; if verb ends in CVC
   with last syllable stressed and final letter not x or w, double

the final consonant and add -ed; if verb ends in Cy, drop the
y before adding -ied; in all other verbs, add -ed.
3) Agent nouns: same rules as past tenses, with r replacing d.
4) Plurals of nouns, third person singular of verbs: if word ends
in s, x, z, ch or sh, add -es; if word ends in Cy, drop y and
add -ies; in all other words, add -s.

This program generated a small number of spurious words such as
ICEMANS.

The list below was extracted from Ritchie's full list of transposals. The quality of each transposal is indicated by a pair of numbers
denoting the number of trigrams and the number of bigrams in common in the two words. Transposals published prior to the computer
list (or discovered independently, although not published) are credited.

17 basiparachromatin - Marsipobranchiata (1,5) Holding, Enigma
Oct 1971

15 cinematographer - megachiropteran (0,2) McPherrin, Enigma
Dec 1927

14 nitromagnesite - regimentations (0,0) Pearce, Enigma Aug 1971
   rotundifoliate - titanofluoride (0,0)
   prerealization - proletarianize (0,2)
   perturbational - protuberantial (0,4)
   pectinesterase - prenecessitate (0,4)
   protomagnesium - spermatogonium (1,2)
   inconglomerate - nongeometrical (2,0) Pearce, Enigma Nov 1974
§ interrogatives - tergiversation (3,0) "The Poser" "Alec Sander",
Ardmore Puzzler Sep 1906

13 aeolharmonica - chloroanaemia (0,1)
   micranthropos - promonarchist (0,1)
   intermorainic - recrimination (0,1) Darryl Francis
   commercialist - microclimates (0,1)
   interoceptors - retrospection (0,1)
   counterpoiser - reprosecution (0,1)
   parasyntheton - thysanopteran (0,2)
   overcirculate - uterocervical (0,2)
   contrarieties - recreationist (0,2)
+ personalistic - pictorialness (0,2) McPherrin, Enigma Nov 1941
   micropetalous - somatopleuric (0,2)
   investigation - tenovaginitis (0,2)
   pedometrician - premedication (0,3)
   superintended - unpredestined (0,3)
   hemicatalepsy - mesaticephaly (0,4)
   iconometrical - intracoelomic (0,4)
* disorientater - sideronatrite (0,4)
   superintender - unenterprised (0,4)
   peridiastolic - proidealistic (0,4)
   hypoglossitis - physiologists (0,5)
   cholesteremia - heteroecismal (1,0)

Deinocephalia - palaeechinoid (1,1)
paraproctitis - participators (1,1)
guarantorship - uranographist (1,1) McPherrin, Enigma Mar 1931
inoperculates - persecutional (1,1)
chlorinations - nonhistorical (1,1)
cephalometric - petrochemical (1,2)
discriminator - doctrinairism (1,2)
protectorates - statoreceptor (1,2)
periprostatic - precipitators (1,2)
* disorientater - endoarteritis (1,2)
* endoarteritis - sideronatrite (1,2)
redintegrator - retrogradient (1,2)
countertrades - unstercorated (1,3)
propraetorial - Protoperlaria (2,1)
condylomatous - monodactylous (2,1)
interceptions - septentrionic (2,2)
cryptostomate - prostatectomy (3,0)

Particular attention should be paid to the three starred pairs which
taken together form a mutually well-mixed transposal trio. Of the
48 transposal pairs printed out by the computer, only 8 had been previously discovered.

To complete the list of well-mixed transposals, it is necessary
to consider those outside the scope of the computer printout -- transposals from other dictionaries, or transposals involving derived
forms of words in Webster's Second (but not in the Collegiate).
The ones given below are added to the list without question.

16 thermonastically - hematocrystallin (1,2) John E. Ogden

15 dechlorinations - ornithoscelidan (0,1) McPherrin, Enigma Jun 1925
   photoresistance - stenocrotaphies (0,5) Holding

14 phonautographs - anthropophagus (0,1) McPherrin, Enigma Jan 1927
   Procrusteanism - superromantics (0,2) Holding
   preconsolation - spironolactone (1,2) Holding

13 acetonitriles - intersocietal (0,0) Francis
   semipectorals - stereoplasmic (0,1) Holding
 + pictorialness - porcelainists (0,1) McPherrin, Enigma Nov 1941
   clypeastroids - perissodactyl (0,1) Holding
   interarcualis - reticularians (0,2) Holding
 = Cinosternidae - containerised (0,2) Holding
   readaptations - tetradiapason (0,3) McPherrin, Enigma Jun 1925
   characterless -clearstarches (0,4) McPherrin, Enigma Mar 1926
   ancylotherium - ethylcoumarin (0,4) Francis
 = Cinosternidae - inconsiderate (0,4) Holding, Enigma Jun 1976
   inspectorates - protestancies (1,0) Holding
 + personalistic - porcelainists (1,0) McPherrin, Enigma Nov 1941
   prenosticates - protestancies (1,2) Holding
 = containerised - inconsiderate (1,2) Holding
   cheiropterans - terpsichorean (1,2) "Sol", Enigma Jul 1934

All words are in Webster's Second except for PORCELAINIST (Funk & Wagnalls Unabridged), OVERREACTION (Random House Unabridged), ANCYLOTHERIUM (Century Dictionary), ETHYLCOUMARIN (Hackh's Chemical Dictionary), and CONTAINERISED (Oxford English Dictionary Supplement, 1972). SUPERROMANTIC is given in a list that does not specify the part of speech; to be pluralized, it must be a noun rather than an adjective. CHIROPTERAN is in Webster's Second, along with the prefix CHEIRO- listed as a variant of CHIRO-. PECTORAL is listed as both an adjective and a noun, although the boldface listing SEMIPECTORAL does not specify the part of speech. DISENCHARM is in Webster's Second, and MERCHANDISING is listed in lightface type there. The singular form of various noun plurals in the above list can be found in boldface in Webster's Second or Third. Two more mutually well-mixed transposal trios are indicated by = and + signs.

Some people may also be willing to admit one or more of the following transposals.

15 nonrealisations - siaresinotannol (0,2) Francis

14 misinterpreted - predeterminist (2,3) "Sue Doe", Enigma Jan 1954
§ reinvestigator - tergiversation (0,3) "Chet", Enigma Jul 1946
§ interrogatives - reinvestigator (2,2) "Chet", Enigma Jul 1946

13 cartelisation - intercostalia (0,1) Francis

NONREALIZATION is found in Webster's Second, and CARTELIZATION in the Random House Unabridged; it may be reasonable to introduce a British spelling for these words, even though unsupported by American dictionaries. PREDETERMINISM and PREDETERMINISTIC can be found in Webster's Unabridged, as can REINVESTIGATE and INVESTIGATOR. The two-word term SPATIA INTERCOSTALIA can be found in Dorland's Medical Dictionary.

If one allows gerundial plurals of words listed in unabridged dictionaries (EDULCERATINGS, REINUNDATINGS) or archaic endings (REINVIGORATEST), further well-mixed transposals are possible. However, a line must be drawn somewhere, or else one will end up admitting such transposals as HYDROCALUMITES - TRICHLAMYDEOUS. The second word appears in a list of isograms compiled by Jack Levine in 1957 from Webster's Unabridged and a variety of specialized dictionaries. A diligent search failed to reveal such a word, although the somewhat similar words MONOCHLAMYDEOUS and DICHLAMYDEOUS do appear. The first word relates to a group of plants in which the flowers have no petals; the second, to a plant with perianth differentiated into a calyx and a corolla. Since botanists apparently do not further subdivide the perianth, the TRI- construction, though orthographically impeccable, does not correspond to reality. In view of the fact that a number of the longest entries in Levine's list are obvious coinages (noisy lumberjack, unwatchdoglike, phantomy figure, etc.), one must regretfully conclude that TRICHLAMYDEOUS is an invention.

<u>State Name Transposals</u>   (Dmitri A. Borgmann)

For the dedicated logologist, it has always been an article of faith that every English word and name can be transposed into some other word or name, or into a cohesive group of words functioning as the equivalent of a single word or name, imparting a unified meaning, clearly and grammatically.

The validity of this belief has never been put to an objective test. Some years ago, I decided to subject this tenet to a critical test, by examining the names of the fifty states of the United States. Considered collectively, these names are as intransigent a set of words as one could ever encounter. The results of my efforts are presented below (transposals followed by an asterisk were discovered by Darryl H. Francis, Hampton, Middlesex, England).

ALABAMA - Taking our cue from the Old Testament, we choose to describe a heathen soothsayer as A BALAAM, which is as good a designation as any.

ALASKA - The Hawaiian Islands (note the contrast in locale) are the habitat of certain shrubs bearing large, edible, red fruit. These shrubs are called AKALAS.

ARIZONA - Here is a state that presents us with a choice. A native of the Azores is an AZORIAN*. The ZONARIA* are a group of mammals including the carnivores and certain ungulates. ARZON-IA* is a girl's name, reported in Mencken's Second Supplement to <u>The American Language</u>.

ARKANSAS - Men such as the famous Hindu philosopher and theologian Sankara (or Shankara), who flourished A.D. 800, are known as SANKARAS. Further, SANSKARA* is a Hindu ceremony that purifies from the taint of sin contracted in the womb, according to the Funk & Wagnalls Unabridged.

CALIFORNIA - It seems self-evident that the principal import of this state is AFRICAN OIL*, and that at least some of its residents have revived the ancient Roman Saturnalia under the updated name of the FORNICALIA.

COLORADO - Consistent with its role as a mining state, Colorado has something of a COAL ODOR about it (Colorado coal?).

CONNECTICUT - A coin in the form of a penny with indentations along its circumference is, naturally, a CUT-CENT COIN. This information comes to us through the courtesy of CONNIE C. CUTT*, whose surname is not too common, though found in England.

DELAWARE - A relatively old word expressing the concept of "to-
ward the sheltered side" is ALEEWARD. More currently, WEAR-
DALE* is the name of a district in Durham, England.

FLORIDA - Secretly published maps of the state show a town at the
bottom of Lake Okeechobee named OLDFAIR. Investigators have
been hindered or FORLAID in their attempts to find the town.

GEORGIA - To comply with logological requirements, the town of
Gorge, in Fremont County, Colorado, was transferred to Iowa,
creating GORGE, IA. Since it had no population to begin with, fer-
rying its inhabitants to their new location in a light, airborne vehi-
cle known as an AEROGIG was very easy.

HAWAII - The central motif of unity-consistency is maintained by
transposing this state name into AWA + IHI. Each of the two words
designates a fish of the Pacific Ocean.

IDAHO - The mystic East beckons to us, as we convert Idaho into
ADHOI*, the name of a town in India, west of Ahmedabad, along the
Tropic of Cancer.

ILLINOIS - The act of dashing or striking against something is referred
to as ILLISION by the cognoscenti.

INDIANA - Is Indiana really formless? That is what its anagram,
ANIDIAN*, tells us!

IOWA - AWIO* Bay is located in the Territory of New Guinea, along
the southern coast of New Britain. Not far away, one of the fourteen
regions of Nauru Island is named AIWO*.

KANSAS - KASSAN* is a town southwest of Samarkand, in Uzbekistan;
ASANSK* is a town northeast of Krasnoyarsk, in west-central Si-
beria. The term NASSAK can be found under the entry for diamond
in the Funk & Wagnalls Unabridged.

KENTUCKY - The haunt of our good friend, KNUT C. KEY, has always
been in the Bluegrass State.

LOUISIANA - Knut's girl friend, Alain, once gambled the entire state
against him in a poker game. When she lost, all he obtained was
ALAIN'S IOU for Louisiana.

MAINE - This state name can be transposed into numerous words and
names. The most common word is AMINE, an organic compound.

The most interesting name is MENAI* Strait. On that strait in
Wales is Anglesey Island, and on that island is a town the name of
which is spelled with 58 letters.

MARYLAND - Near the western coast of Australia there stands a
hill 1230 feet high: MARLANDY* Hill. Perched at its summit we
find a wizened old man: DR. LAYMAN (a name affording an interesting contrast, if you stop to think about it!).

MASSACHUSETTS - Have you noticed the hairy upper lips of Russian
news agency representatives? These are TASS MUSTACHES, of
course! Certain specific states which chasms find themselves oc-
cupying, incidentally, are known as CHASM STATUSES*.

MICHIGAN - There go the bells again, A-CHIMING all day long . . .

MINNESOTA - Like a chameleon, this name can twist itself into many
forms, the most elegant transposal being into NOMINATES. Other
rearrangements include MAINSTONE*, a town in Shropshire, England; ANTINOMES, metaphysical contradictories; MONTANISE, to
adhere to Montanism, in ecclesiastical history; ANTIMESON, the
antimatter counterpart of the meson, a subatomic particle; MINNE-
OTAS*, towns such as Minneota, in Lyon County, Minnesota; MAN-
NITOSE, a kind of levulose; MOST INANE, the superlative form of
the adjective inane; and NONSAMITE, any material not the heavy
silk fabric called samite.

MISSISSIPPI - The word ipseity is defined as selfhood. In analogy to
the word solipsism, there must exist the alternative form ipsism.
(As a matter of fact, it does exist, given in medical dictionaries
with a somewhat different meaning.) One way of intensifying the
meaning of a word in English is to double the first part of it --
consider examples such as supersuperior, great-great-grandfather,
and the late late show on TV. Accordingly, we discover that conditions of super-selfhood are known as IPSI-IPSISMS.

MISSOURI - That form of the worship of Osiris now running rampant
among members of the upper class in Great Britain is coming to be
called U OSIRISM. Some of the worshipers have crossed the ocean
and founded the stellar community of SIRIUS, MO.

MONTANA - This state was apparently first settled by emigrants from
MANATON*, a town in Devonshire, England.

NEBRASKA - There is an ecclesiastical district in southeast Devonshire by the name of BRANKSEA*. Webster's Second reveals that BANKERAS* are stone curlews of Santo Domingo.

NEVADA - The carful of transpositions to which this state name lends itself includes VENADA, another name for the pudu, a deer; VE-DANA, a term for sensation in Buddhism; and ADAVEN, a community in Nye County, Nevada which can be combined with the state name to produce a 12-letter palindrome: Adaven, Nevada.

NEW HAMPSHIRE - During her recent trip to London, HERMINE P. SHAW examined SERAPHIM-HEWN* statues in what might be called an EPHRAIM-SHEWN museum; that is, the guide who conducted her on a tour through the museum was named Ephraim.

NEW JERSEY - Does J.R. SWEENEY live in New Jersey? If he does, and if he has been seen by the Jewish population of that state, we can refer to him as JEWRY-SEEN*.

NEW MEXICO - Should we walk down the street and meet an undetermined number of women substituting for icemen, we might have to describe them as " X" ICEWOMEN.

NEW YORK - An old form of the past participle of the verb wreak, now occupied by the word wrought, is Y-WROKEN*. If this seems too esoteric, consider the word KEY-WORN: worn out by overuse of a key, said of keyholes. So saith ROY KEWN*, anyway.

NORTH CAROLINA - Can you visualize NORA I. CHARLTON* holding aloft A LOCRIAN THORN? If you can, then you will also understand why ornithologists need a word defined as "relating to sensuality in birds". That word is, of course, ORNITHOCARNAL*.

NORTH DAKOTA - This state is the legal residence of one DORA K. HATTON.

OHIO - Until recently, there existed a surname HOOI* in the London Telephone Directory. This is also the sound made by wind whistling round a corner or through a keyhole, according to the English Dialect Dictionary.

OKLAHOMA - This may be transposed into the short phrase A HOLM OAK, a dictionary entry in Webster's Second.

OREGON - One who has the determination to go on in the face of adversity is either an ONGOER (compare onlooker) or a GOER-ON

(compare hanger-on). More prosaically, ORGONE* is the name
of a vital energy held to pervade nature and to be accumulable for
use by the human body by sitting in a specially designed box (see
Webster's Third Edition).

PENNSYLVANIA - Did you ever hear of a plastic floor covering so
thin that it quivers like a leaf? We call it AN ASPEN VINYL.

RHODE ISLAND - If HILDA D. ROSEN lives in Rhode Island, she must
know that it is a SHOAL-RIDDEN land, especially the district around
OLD SHERIDAN*, a town shown on the same secret maps that have
given us Oldfair, Florida. In a different vein, it seems perfectly
logical that the correlative of a foot soldier is a HAND SOLDIER.

SOUTH CAROLINA - If there is a song entitled "South Carolina" --
and there may well be one -- would you say that a LAOTIAN CHOR-
US* singing it would consistute A RASH LOCUTION?

SOUTH DAKOTA - This state symbolizes the wise, old owl, in the
form of A HOOT AT DUSK.

TENNESSEE - That special brand of common sense peculiar to teen-
agers is known as TEEN SENSE. Those endowed with it describe
young birds placed in nests as ENNESTEES.

TEXAS - The simplest transposal of this name is into TAXES. Far
more elegantly, we have SEXTA, a feminine first name.

UTAH - An old word for height is HAUT. AHUT* is a fourteenth-cen-
tury spelling of aught in the Oxford English Dictionary. The 23rd
letter of the Hebrew alphabet is sometimes spelled THAU*.

VERMONT - Any man whose name is Victor Merton will, undoubtedly, wish to sign it as V. MERTON*, and to have it so listed in
the telephone directory. During his stay in London, the Italian-
English music composer Matthias Vento must surely have been
addressed as MR. VENTO.

VIRGINIA - The tree genus IRVINGIA is listed in Funk & Wagnalls
Unabridged.

WASHINGTON - SNOW-HATING Washington saw nothing NOWA-
NIGHTS. (Try working up a sentence like that for each of the
other states!)

WEST VIRGINIA - A gentleman by the name of IRVING WAITES* has pointed out to us that the name of this state can be rearranged into the adjective STAIR-VIEWING.

WISCONSIN - Since Wisconsin is the Dairy State, it is fitting to think about its cattle population. The puritanical view holds that, without benefit of clergy, what the state has is COWS IN SIN.

WYOMING - Taking the word y-wroken previously mentioned in connection with New York as our model, we see in Wyoming the present participle Y-MOWING. Such, at any rate, is the claim of our informant, IO M. GWYN.

THE TWO RAVENS

For years, poets and writers have experimented with a wide variety of literary constraints upon their compositions: lipograms, in which a letter is consistently omitted; acrostics, in which the initial letters of each line of a poem spell out a word or phrase; and (more recently) palindromes, in which the letters of a poem or story spell out the same message when read in reverse. Some constraints (lipograms) are relatively weak, allowing many different ways of telling a story; others (palindromes) are so strong that it is almost impossible to get a given story across to the reader. These differences can be clearly illustrated by two attempts to recreate an unconstrained literary work in constrained form: Edgar Allan Poe's well-known poem "The Raven".

The Acrostic Raven

Howard Bergerson of Sweet Home, Oregon has modified the acrostic poem by requiring that the initial letters of each word in the poem spell out a message. Further, he has turned the poem in on itself by requiring that this message not be an arbitrary one, but the first part of the same poem, as in

> Blue Lovebirds
> Under Evening's Large Orb
> Vow Eternal Byronic Imprinting ...

and the next word must begin with the letter R.

This restriction is a fairly severe one, so much so that he could preserve the story-line of "The Raven", but little of the rhyme-scheme and none of the meter. Nevertheless, it does capture the eeriness of the original fairly well.

Midnight intombed December's naked icebound gulf.
Haggard, tired, I nodded, toiling over my books.
Eldritch daguerreotyped dank editions cluttered even my bed;
Exhaustion reigned.
Suddenly, now, a knocking, echoing door I cognized:
"Eminent Boreas, open up no door!
Go, uninvited lonely frigid haunt!
Avaunt, grim guest -- and roar!"

Distinctly, too, I remember
Embers dwindling into numinous orange death.
Delving elaborately, desiring tomorrow overmuch,
I labored -- ineffectually numbing grief.
Outre volumes eloquently retrogressed my yearning --
Brooding on olden knowledge sorrowfully evoked Lenore!
Death's Regent, inscrutable, tragically called her --
Damsel a Godhead Unspeakable elected, rare radiant, evermore!

Overhearing the yawning purple effluent drapes
Discreetly and nebulously kissing,
Electrified, delusively in terror, I overassessed nocturnal susurruses.
Curtain language utterances? The threshold's eerie rappings ensued! --
Darkness engendered visitations ethereal!
Nonetheless, my yellowed but ember-lit door
(Eddying xanthic hues and ushered shadows teeming!)
I opened not -- really expecting itinerant guests not evermore.

Dredging strength up, drumming determination eclipsed,
Nor lamely yielding, nor obeying weakness anew,
Knowing no occult caller knocked, I negotiated gently:
"Evident caller, honored one, I've napped -- grown dreamy -- over-
        looking obvious rappings."
I careened outside, gazed nonplussed in zigzag, everchanging directions.
Elusive music in night's emptiness nascent tempests bore.
Only rifted escarpments and shivering openness proved evident.
Newcomers unheralded probed no open door!

Out over ruinous gapings of umbral Night
I noticed voices, I thought -- ephemeral, distant, lilting ones now --
Enunciating "Lenore." Yet, fearfully rigid, I gazed.
I'd definitely heard an unearthly nuance
Tremble across voids abysmal.
Understanding narrowed! Terrors, goblin riding, inundated me galore!
Uncannily, echoes spoke, too, a name!
Did reason o'ercloud afore?

Returning, distraught, inside,
Soon then I noted continued tappings louder yet --
Tympanic obbligatos ominous, I readily each magnified,
Envisioning menacing but exalted ranks enveloping me:
" But explanation requires something!
Dark windows in nival dwellings -- lattices -- improvising noises galore
In namings, tappings! Onomatopoeia?
Nothing -- understandably -- more?"

I nimbly opened up shutters -- opened rationality also,
Not giving extravagant dubieties even a thought.
Hopping dignifiedly -- even ludicrously vain --
In, now, galumphed, eyes lustering, a black old raven.
Aloft this ebon luminary yawed -- doorframes

Evidently serve invading ravens, if nests galore
Tumble out midnight's outrageous riotous reach of wind,
Ousting vultures even -- ravens more.

Unceremoniousness calms heartache. I laughed aloud:
" Black old raven, exiting December's inkiest night, ebon feathers
      fluttering,
Establish courtly tenure unconditionally -- announce, lofty lord, your
      name!
Utter, mysterious bird, <u>incomprehensible</u> names! -- given good rebi,
      I'll explore!"
Full obligingly uninhibited, the raven,
Employing vocal organs loudly, unsettling my ears,
Spake, exclaimed, lilted, opined,
Quoth, uttered even, "Nevermore!"

The lamplight's yellow radiance enshrouded the raven.
Ornithic genius rarely exists;
Substantiated, such excellence dazzled me:
" Ye, yclept elegantly, answered -- reciting nobly --
Inspired nonsense, gifted bird!
Roost overhead on door,"
I nodded genially; "oddball nuns of long-vanished days
Even named knaves 'Nevermore!'"

One weirdly lamenting, ego denting, ghastly, ever so old raven
Reserving one word for utterance!
Largely limited, yet enviable vocabulary
Oozing knowledge epicureans deplore!
" Likely enough, nightmarish old ravens eventually depart,
Empathies abandoning."
The hollow sounding raven, emptily gargling echoes,
Now trebled inanely, "Nevermore!"

Startled categorically, reeling under this astounding bird,
" Likely enough, this reply aptly given," I concluded,
" Acquired laboriously, like yoga,
Comprises all lexicological loot ever delivered him.
Even ravens distill a master's sadness,
Emitting loquaciously agonies galore.
Obviously delirious, his erstwhile almoner
Doggedly ululated, 'Nevermore!'"

Smiles -- perhaps evanescent amusement -- kindling,
A bird luxuriantly ebon ejecting lorn exotic cries
Teases even dullards. Reclining and reasoning esoterically,
Reviewing arcane dialectics, I argued necessitously
This enigmatic, villianous, eccentric raven's meaning,
Oft repeated eloquently o'er.
" Vaunted egotistical raven, have elsewhither's avians raptorial
Inveighed, 'Nevermore'?"

Guessing thus -- hushed, expressionlessly, yielding audible words not,
I nuzzled gorgeous pillows umbilically, rich purple lining embracing.
Exultant, foul, fiery, luciferous, unholy eyes now the dread raven
      aimed piercingly --
Eyes starkly depraved!
I snuggled, cushioned, reclining, emptily enduring the lamplight's
      yearning avidity.
Neither doing nor expiring. But uprisen Lenore --
Oh unclaspable shade! -- longingly, yea, knew I
She shall irradiate -- nevermore!

Gratifying ears, lungs engorging, came tinklings ribboned in fragrance!
I expected divinities delivering ease long unfelt!
"Sneak," I vituperated, "ethereal Lenore you'd irreverently nullify,
Threatening every revered remembrance of rapture I own!
Vile emissary -- raven angels secretively sent,
Exacerbating sadness sore --
Embitterer, drink nectarous oblivion!"
Croaked the ugly raven, "Nevermore!"

"Archfiendish leerer!
Seer unholy! --
Sent up rockshafts, rifts, upwhirling storms, enchanted sands,--
Charismatically usurping -- ravaging this abode,
Is nostalgic love's assuagement nicknamed Gilead? --
Unutterable assuagement galore?
Elucidate! Unbosom thyself!"
The evil raven answered, "Nevermore!"

"Confess, evil seer, the Hereafter exists!
This heart remorseful eventually shall hold omniabsent Lenore!
Deity Supreme even evil ravens intuit -- evil ravens adore!
Peculiarly prescient individual, now glowering strangely -- eyeing noth-
      ingness, -- seer unholy! --
Eternity's Damozel Divine acknowledge,
Repudiating kind nepenthe's eventless sleep!
Seer -- evil nonetheless -- grant Eternity's numinous Damozel exists --
Remote, ethereal, divine!
Verily, I sadly implore!"
The avian troll imprecated orally, "Nevermore!"

"Satanic emissary, that horrible edict represents excommunication!
Adieu! Leave now on night's elemental tempest! --
Hurtling endlessly! -- liquidating Evil's syrinx sheerly!
Midst yearning (yes, excruciating loneliness), liar of winter's empti-
      ness -- depart!
Begone up that egress, mephistophelian bird!
(Enter, radiant Lenore, invisibly!)"
The detestably ogreish old raven -- eyes demoniacally dreaming --
Yawped inimically, "Nevermore!"

Glow xanthic and nauseous, thou horrendous illuming chandelier!
High up, ensconced still, always nictitating dourly,
Umbral shadow hurl earthward, raven!
Ever deepening shadow,
Hover -- as down on waters Stygian!
Thus escape evades me. Imagination's necrotic gore
I've obviated,
Prayerfully expecting new ecstatic dawnings -- nevermore!

The Heteroliteral Raven

In a heteroliteral poem, each pair of successive words is required
to have no letters in common. This is a considerably weaker constraint, as can be seen from the fact that it was possible to retain
the rhyme-scheme and meter of the original poem as well as the
story line.

On a midnight, cool and foggy, as I pondered, light and groggy,
Ancient books and musty ledgers, not remembered any more,
As I nodded, all but napping, there I sensed a muffled tapping,
Very much a hushful rapping, just behind my attic door.
"'Tis a guest, mayhap," I muttered, "knocking at my attic door --
    I can't judge it's any more."

Ah, so well I can remember, it was in the wan December,
As I saw the dying ember flash red light upon the floor;
Wishing for a sunny morrow, in my writings could I borrow
Any surcease of my sorrow? -- pain so keen for my Lenore?
Ah, so fair, so cheerful vision, called to heaven, my Lenore,
    Away from us forevermore.

But a flutter, so uncertain, of my deep-red wall of curtain
Woke in me fantastic horror, cutting deeply to my core;
Shall it end, this crazy tumble of my heart? -- I then did mumble,
"'Tis a visitor, and humble, knocking at my attic door --
'Tis a person, caught by darkness, who raps on my attic door.
    That is all -- none might say more."

In a while, my will much stronger, I soon faltered no bit longer;
"Miss, or laddie," soft I murmured, "this long wait one must deplore,
But I had been softly napping; much too feeble was your tapping,
Very faint you fell to rapping, well upon my attic door.
Then I was not sure I heard you --" here I opened attic door;
    Night saw I but no sight more.

In my outer hallway peering, stood I long there, dumbly fearing;
Much in doubt, I soon had visions that nobody saw before;
It was quiet, all unbroken; magic lull gave not a token;
Was the word that I had spoken, rubric of the maid Lenore?
This, a whisper, and it echoed, murmur, like a kiss, "Lenore".
    This alone -- but no bit more.

Back in chamber, slow returning, all my soul within me burning,
Yet again the sound I noted -- was it louder than before? --
I now cried, "A noisy rat is out behind my birch wood lattice;
Soon I shall detect if that is true -- a puzzle fast explore;
Ah, my heart, do rest a trifle and this puzzle fast explore --
      It's a wind, but no bit more."

Plucky, I unlatched my shutter, and, with saucy flirt and flutter,
In flew quick a lofty Raven, of a long-lost day before.
Such a lordly snub he paid me! proud, with beak up, not afraid, he
Sprang with grace of duke or lady onto rim of attic door;
Sat upon a bust of Pallas, on the rim of attic door;
      Haughty pride -- but no bit more.

Such a dusky crow beguiling my dour fancy to be smiling
By its glum and stiff decorum, by the pious face it wore,
"Bald your pate is, cut or shaven; you," I spake, "you aren't so craven,
Old, repugnant owlish raven, fowl dispatched from windy shore:
Quick, reveal thy public nomen, quick, yet from a dim-lit shore!"
      It crowed flatly, "Nevermore."

Full I marveled how ungainly, crested fowl did talk so plainly,
Though I saw no wit or meaning, or a hint of avian lore;
But we may not duck agreeing how a child or adult being
Has no luck of truly seeing fowl perched full on attic door
      Naming self a "Nevermore."

But yon bird, aloof but lonely, sat upon my door, said only
That glum word -- a grieving soul in that glum word he did outpour.
In a lull, I heard no utter; pinions flat, I saw no flutter;
I then said -- my voice a mutter -- "No dear soul did stay before;
In the dawn he will be missing -- hope did flee away before --"
      It now did say "Nevermore."

I, aghast by calm thus broken with reply so fitly spoken,
Glumly said, "The word it mumbled is a summit of its lore.
Caught from his unlucky master who, alas, knew much Disaster,
Gloom sensed quickly, ever-faster, no bird songs he can outpour --
All is gloom, is melancholy; but one lay he can outpour,
      A dirge so wailful: 'Nevermore'."

As yon bird yet was beguiling my dour fancy to be smiling,
Drew I up my chair of velvet, facing bust and fowl at door;
In my cushion's velvet sinking, warmly occupied by linking
Daydream unto daydream, thinking deeply, I perused my core:
What could this fowl mean, I quavered, looking deep within my core,
      As it crowed that "Nevermore"?

I was occupied by guessing what or why, no fact expressing
To my bird, whose burning eyes now glared on me atop my door;
This and more I sat divining, as my head now sat reclining

Fast upon a soft red lining, that yon lamp does light up more,
Lining on my chair so ruddy, that yon lamp does light up more --
       Will she warm it? Nevermore!

I breathed in: the air got denser, balm of spice from pallid censer
Hid by seraphim of Heaven, softly pacing o'er my floor.
"Dunce," I called, "Thy God has lent you -- he's by pungent odor
       sent you
Respite -- balm which may prevent you pining for thy maid, Lenore!
Quaff, oh quaff this cup so magic, shun all hints of thy Lenore!"
       It crowed flatly, "Nevermore."

"Pithy augur -- thing of evil! -- augur yet, if beast or devil!
From a Tempter did you flee, or did a storm place you at shore?
I see you are cool, undaunted by this cubby so enchanted,
By this dreadful spot, all haunted; for me croak thy cunning lore --
Can I yet find balm of Gilead? -- oh, divulge thy cunning lore!"
       It crowed flatly, "Nevermore."

"Pithy augur -- thing of evil! -- augur yet, if beast or devil!
By our Heaven up on high, or by that God we must adore,
Will, perhaps, I, sorrow-laden, if placed in the land of Aidenn,
Hug a bright and holy maiden who I honor as Lenore:
Hug, ecstatic, my lost maiden who I honor as Lenore?"
       It crowed flatly, "Nevermore."

"Such a word's a sign of parting, fowl debased!" I howled, upstarting:
"Go, return, fly through a whirlwind to a rocky dim-lit shore!
Quill or plume, I shun all token -- gaudy lies thy soul hath spoken --
I ask quiet, all unbroken; fly now, quit my attic door!
Take your beak from in my heart; so fly now, quit my attic door!"
       It crowed flatly, "Nevermore."

I can see that bird now sitting by the lamp -- no upward flitting --
Perched on pallid bust of Pallas right above my attic door,
His two eyes now ruddy, gleaming just like Satan's, wholly dreaming
By the lamp which, softly beaming, throws dim shafts upon my floor:
And my soul, pinned fast in shadow flung across my attic floor,
       Can rise up, ah, nevermore!

LINGUISTS AT PLAY

Superl (Charles Elliott)

Word Ways readers may be interested in the contents of the following letter recently received from the Division of Unusual Languages of
the United States Coast Guard at Varna, N.Y. I quote it in full:

Your request for information (writes Lieutenant Commander Boeth-
ius C. Heminstitch, the Public Relations Officer of the Division) about
SUPERL has been forwarded to me. I hope that you will not take of-
fense because I have not used SUPERL in this letter; it has been a long-
standing policy of this office to answer all requests in the language of
the request.

As you probably already know, SUPERL is a language devised to
replace all of the so-called 'natural' languages. It is streamlined and
rationally designed, and has every advantage over the 'natural' languages.

SUPERL was developed by a team of U.S. Coast Guard linguists on
an abandoned oil-rig off Santa Barbara. The Coast Guard sponsored
this research and development project for obvious reasons having to do
with inter-service funding. The project stretched over a period of six
months, and resulted in Coast Guard Handbooks in SUPERL Grammar,
SUPERL Phonology, and SUPERL Readers I and II. At present an ex-
haustive SUPERL Dictionary is under preparation. Over 500 centers
for teaching SUPERL have been established, and it is already the official language of various government departments.

The advantages of SUPERL are many. Using it, speakers may
talk directly in mathematics, physics, chemistry, spherical trigono-
metry, and anthropology, without the necessity of an intervening language. It, of course, makes direct conversion of the foot-pound-Fah-
renheit system to the metric-centigrade system, thus relieving users
of laborious and time-consuming computations. In its binary mode,
SUPERL may be used directly with computers, bypassing any computer languages. With SUPERL a Thesaurus is unnecessary; an
alphabetical listing is a Thesaurus. Thus real relationships of concepts are phonologically represented, and the unwholesome arbitrari-

ness of phonetic symbolization is done away with.

The articulation of SUPERL involves additional facial muscles, so that it is impossible to say something illogical in SUPERL without at least a weak smile. Blatant absurdities result in broad grins and repeated winks.

However, while these are major advantages, they might be built into 'natural' languages. SUPERL has, in addition, two characteristics which no 'natural' language has: truth and compactness.

Grammatical utterances in SUPERL are always true. Thus, new truths about the universe can be discovered by babbling. This has obvious advantages. Speakers of SUPERL have at their tongue-tip (so to speak) the combined knowledge of mankind, and, what is more, all the facts about the universe that they will ever need. The Coast Guard is presently exploiting this characteristic in a unique project. Thirty garrulous people have been gathered in our laboratory in Peoria and instructed to talk about whatever interests them. What they say is recorded, and will be compiled into the SUPERL Encyclopedia. We modestly hope that ultimately this will be the Ultimate Compendium of All Knowledge. If it is declassified, it may prove of interest to scholars and teachers.

SUPERL is, in addition, amazingly compact. What may be a lengthy exegesis in a 'natural' language is often a simple sentence in SUPERL. A classic example of this is B.A. Booper's refutation of Stratificational Analysis. It was a single word! (The word also carried the meaning 'natural waste', but that is neither here nor there.) Whole novels have been written on the back of Howard Johnson menus. SUPERL lends itself quite naturally to poetry. For example,

> Gnuj
> Wroj

shows a height of lyricism not often attained in awkward natural languages. The approximate English translation is "As the moon casts silvery fingers (or greasy forks) over the spider's (or lampshade's, or fodder's) back, does he (or the moon) care, really care? I will return (or become nauseous) to my beloved (or the general public). Is there any other way? (or Do you have any oranges?)" The entire works of Shakespeare are being translated into SUPERL; the result is expected to be a single trilogy of plays. There may be some difficulties with actual production, for, as one writer observed, "The cast is large, but the soliloquies are short."

In spite of the many advantages of SUPERL, large numbers of

people still sullenly refuse to say anything in SUPERL. We guess
that this may be the result of half-baked rumors and spurious opinions
about SUPERL. It would be well to straighten out a few expressions
of anti-SUPERL sentiment.

Some object because speakers seem to be unable to make jokes in
SUPERL. This seems to be a rather pointless objection. Jokes have
their place, but there are all sorts of practical jokes that don't require any use of language at all. Let those who cite this as an objection
stitch a friend's trouser-legs together, or pour olive oil in their wives'
cocktail glasses. In any case, to satisfy these spoil-sports, we may
point out that already a team of United States Coast Guard Transmogri-
ficational Grammarians are already at work devising a set of standard
jokes that may be recited in SUPERL.

That chimps seem to be able to learn SUPERL faster and better
than human beings is not really an objection to the language, either.
There is simply a difference between the brains of chimps and the
brains of human beings. Vive la difference!

The rumor that a recent anthropological finding, an artifact, had
no name in SUPERL and that proponents of SUPERL subsequently
smashed and disposed of the artifact, has no truth in it. Speakers of
SUPERL have tested this rumor by trying to repeat it in SUPERL.
They were able to repeat the rumor, but only with broad grins and
guffaws. Thus, even if true, the rumor had to be most illogical.

The most vicious rumor is that it is possible to say " The world
is coming to an end soon" in SUPERL without even the hint of a smile.
This we must simply discount. If the present trend of diversity in
natural languages continues to pollute our linguistic atmosphere, we
really are in for trouble. Let the anti-SUPERLites consider that,
instead of carping at a minor inconsistency in SUPERL.

I hope I have given you the information you require. You may be
amused to know that there are dirty words in SUPERL. However, in
the interests of National Security, these words have been classified
and may be used only by the highest echelons of the government and
military.

Please write to me directly if you are in need of further information about SUPERL. I would also be grateful if you would forward to
me the names of any you hear being critical of SUPERL. Please indicate in your report whether they are of draft age, or whether they
are supported by any government monies.

The Language Game   (Philip M. Cohen)

Everybody knows of English English, American English, and Pidgin English. Many know of dialects of other languages, such as High and Low German, or Lake and Bodega Miwok. However, certain obscurer dialects are harder to find in the literature: Alto Saxon, for instance, or Super Yuman. The Cornell Linguistics Circle has prepared a list of some of these lesser-known dialects.

Darkest Afrikaans	Brim Fula	Shoo-Fly Paiute
No One Ainu	Howling Gaelic	Bosom Pali
Briar Apache	Natural Gascon	Another Man's Persian
Half Assamese	Gorgeous Georgian	Nail Polish
Dirty Attic	Wheat German	Fools Russian
Lobster Basque	Fenu Greek	Shifting Sanskrit
Vulgar Bulgar	Sea Gullah	Canna Sardinian
Alley Catalan	Full Hausa	Alto Saxon
Traffic Coptic	Cornish Hindi	Hop Scottish
Pop Cornish	Bunny Hopi	Original Seneca
Derniere Cree	Taket Izi	George Bernard Shawnee
Upper Creek	Overhead Kham	Worcester Sherpa
Shrimp Creole	Swift Kickapoo	Hot Somali
Rubber Czech	Terpsi Korean	Sickeningly Swedish
Prune Danish	Over Kota	Dwomedary Tamil
Cellar Doric	Flight Kru	White Thai
Going Dutch	Ge Latin	Pidgin Toda
Protestant Efik	Iceberg Lettish	Thanksgiving Turkic
Wetten Erse	Stove Lydian	Christmas Twi
Gall Estonian	Edna St. Vincent Malay	Whooping Ukrainian
Itch Etruscan	Chocolate Maltese	Electric Ute
Photo Finnish	Gentle Mandarin	Wishing Welsh
Nasal Flemish	Coal Mayan	Resounding Walapai
Best French	Three Blind Mycenean	Super Yuman
Deep Frisian	Euph Oriya	Bronx Zulu

Dave Silverman of West Los Angeles, California, Daniel Bial of Summit, New Jersey, R. Robinson Rowe of Sacramento, California, Harry Hazard of Rochester, New York and James Rambo of Palo Alto, California added many more:

Mortal Annamese	Standing Horvation
Ding Bats	Gnawing Hungarian
Berber of Seville	Rikki Tikki Kavi
Hill Bhili	Proto Kol
Bheli Bhutanese	A Kpelle

Strawberry Cham
Double Chin
Checkered Chinese
Blue Chippewa
Gottingen Dutch

Body English
Reverse English
Rolling Estonian
Rotary Fan
Extrava Ganza

Fee Garo
Cousin German
Indira Gondi
Milwauk Hebrew
Westward Ho

Chocolate Kuki
Stand-up Kumyk
National Lampong
Last Lapp
Anti Makasser

Virgin Maori
Night Norse
Stand Patois
Love Phocian
Yo Semitic

Dying Svan
Dotted Swiss
Hot Tumali
Cry Wolof
Snarley Yao

Of these, Snarley Yao requires explanation: snarleyyow is a word in Webster's Second Unabridged much prized by logologists for its double Y.

Daniel Bial, noting that Pidgin Toda on the first list incorporates two languages, added Cree Sus, and another is Fox Fur.

WORD SQUARES

A word square is a square array of letters forming words in both the horizontal and vertical directions: a miniature crossword puzzle with no blacked-in squares. There are two basic types, the regular word square in which the same set of words appears both horizontally and vertically, and the double word square in which the vertical and horizontal words are different. For squares of a particular size, double word squares are more difficult to find than regular ones.

Word squares have been actively studied for at least a century, principally by members of the National Puzzlers' League and similar puzzleistic organizations in the United States. Much effort was devoted to finding large word squares, and today it is generally conceded that an eight-by-eight regular word square and a seven-by-seven double word square are the largest ones constructible with words drawn entirely from Webster's Second or Third Unabridged Dictionary. To construct larger squares, it has been necessary to collect word lists from a wide variety of sources -- dialect dictionaries, gazetteers, biographical dictionaries and the like. Experience has shown that it is better to construct squares from the bottom up rather than from the top down, in order to preserve as many options as possible as the work proceeds. Therefore, such lists were generally prepared in reverse-alphabetical form, alphabetized by terminal letter instead of initial one. Most lists were generated in handwritten or typewritten form only, and few copies of these are extant.

With the advent of the high-speed digital computer, new vistas have opened for the logologist. Because of the immense number of combinatorial possibilities, it has been impossible to check by hand all possible sets of n-letter words in a list to see whether a square could be formed. Even a computer cannot do this in a reasonable time, but it can be programmed to check many more promising leads than a human can. Two problems, however, remain: computing, although steadily falling in price, can still be expensive, and handwritten or typewritten word lists must be converted into a form the machine can read.

Six-by-Six Double Word Squares by Computer

The potential of the computer for finding unsuspected word squares has been dramatically demonstrated by M. D. McIlroy of Bernardsville, New Jersey using a Bell Telephone Laboratories computer. Prior to 1976, few if any six-by-six double word squares using common words were known; in Language on Vacation (Scribner's, 1965), Dmitri Borgmann cites the following square as one of the better ones.

Although all the words appear in Webster's
Second Unabridged, four (ectene, adiate,
pirite, adance) do not appear in the Collegiate, and two others are derived forms not
in boldface there.

```
S A P P E R
A D I A T E
M A R T H A
U N I T E R
E C T E N E
L E E R E D
```

Restricting himself to words in boldface
in Webster's Collegiate (not even allowing inferred plurals of nouns,
or inferred verb past tenses or gerunds), McIlroy instructed the
machine to search for six-by-six double word squares. To his surprise, 117 different squares were revealed, including several in
which eleven of the twelve different words were in Webster's Pocket
Dictionary. (The twelfth word was ratton, a dialect version of "rat",
in some squares and Avesta, the sacred books of Zoroastrianism, in
others.)

Several of these word squares occur in clusters which are described separately from the main listing. The most notable cluster
has seventeen squares which can be divided into two slightly different
groups of 12 and 5 squares, respectively:

```
S C H I S +      Replace * with        PA  PI  TA  TA
* R * N C E      any of following:     T   T   P   F
R A T T O N
I N T E N +      Replace + with        M   T   T
* I E R C E      any of following:     D   D   T
E A R N E R
```

```
S U F I S M      Replace * with        PA  PI  TA  TA  TA
* R * N C E      any of following:     T   T   F   P   P
R A T T O N                           ER  ER  ER  ER  TN
I N T E N D
* I E R C E
* A * N E R
```

Three smaller clusters of five, three and two squares, respectively,
are given below:

```
* A S * E R      Replace * with        C   T   C   T   C   T   C   T   G   S
* U * * L E      any of following:     LCI LCI LNU RTI RTI
U R O P O D                            RD  ST  RD  ST  ST
T O R P I D
C R E E S E
H A * * E N
```

```
D E S P O T      Replace * with        O   A   A
I N H U M E      any of following:     RM  RM  NT
S C * R E R
H A V I N G
E G E S T A
D E * * A L
```

```
L A S S O S      Replace * with      C T
E S C A P E      any of following:   D P
C L O * H E
T O R R I D
O P I A T E
R E A * E R
```

Twenty-four of the remaining 90 squares are given below.

```
H A M A T E      H E G I R A      H O T T E R      J I G S A W
I S A B E L      E V A D E R      U R E I D E      U N L A C E
S P O R E D      R E S E N T      M I S S I S      S T A N C E
P I R A T E      E N S A T E      P O T A T O      T E D D E D
I R I D E S      T E E T E R      E L I N O R      U N L A D E
D E S E R T      O R R E R Y      D E S E R T      S T Y L E R


K I R S C H      L E A V E S      L E P T U S      M I S S U S
I N H E R E      E X T E R N      E S S E N E      O R P I N E
S H I N E R      D H A R M A      S C O T I A      R E I V E R
M A N N E D      G A M B I R      S A C R A L      U N L I V E
E L O I S E      E L A I N E      O P I A T E      L I T T E N
T E S T E R      R E N D E R      R E D D E R      A C H E N E


N E W I S H      O M A H A S      P A R A P H      P A R A P H
U R A N I A      M I L I E U      A C A C I A      A V U L S E
T R I V E T      A S T E R N      S C I E N T      R E D D E R
L A T E N T      S H A M A N      S E S T E T      I N D I U M
E T E R N E      U N I A T E      I D E A T E      A G E N D A
T A R T A R      M A C L E D      M E D L A R      H E R E O N


P A S S I M      P A T T E R      P E L O P S      P H A S I C
O R I O D E      E Q U A T E      O R A C L E      L A C U N A
T E A S E R      T U S C H E      T A R T A N      A M E N D S
A O R T A L      R I C T A L      A S K A N T      N U T L E T
S L E E T Y      E L A I N E      T E E N E R      E L A I N E
H E R R E N      L A N C E R      O R R E R Y      T I L T E R


P O S A D A      P R I M A L      R A B A T O      R A C I S M
T R O G O N      R E C I P E      E L O P E R      A P O G E E
O O L O N G      O T I T I S      S U L L E N      P E N N I A
S I G N A L      S E C R E T      O L E I N E      I R V I N G
I D E A T E      E N L A C E      R A T T E R      S C O T E R
S E L L E R      R E E L E R      B R I E R Y      T U Y E R E


R A C I S M      R A D U L A      R A F T E R      R A G M A N
E V I N C E      O S I R I S      I L L I T E      E M E U T E
P E R S O N      A S S E S S      C L O T H E      C E N T R A
A S C E N T      M U T A T E      H E R B A L      A L T A I R
S T U C C O      E R A S E R      E L A I N E      L I E N A L
T A S T E R      R E L E N T      N E S T E R      L A S T L Y
```

The Search for a Ten-by-Ten Word Square

How good a job can a computer do searching for larger squares ?
Using a list of 35,000 boldface words in Webster's Second Unabridged,
Frank Rubin of Wappingers Falls, New York instructed a computer to
look for a ten-by-ten regular word square. Although previous experience suggested that a considerably larger list would be necessary to

```
A  C  C  O  M  P  L  I  S  H
C  O  O  P  E  R  A  N  C  Y
C  O  P  A  T  E  N  T  E  E
O  P  A  L  E  S  C  E  N  T
M  E  T  E  N  T  E  R  O  N
P  R  E  S  T  A  T  I  O  N
L  A  N  C  E  T  O  O  T  H
I  N  T  E  R  I  O  R  L  Y
S  C  E  N  O  O  T  L
H  Y  E  T  N  N  H  Y
```

find such a square, the computer did remarkably well, finding words
for eight out of the ten lines. (The word lancetooth is a two-word entry
in Webster's Second Unabridged, but is hyphenated in Funk & Wagnalls
Unabridged.)

Dmitri Borgmann of Dayton, Washington and Darryl Francis of
Hampton, Middlesex, England approached the ten-by-ten word square
problem from a different angle. Since five-by-five squares are quite
easy to construct, they reasoned that a ten-by-ten square composed
entirely of tautonyms (words such as chimachima and quinaquina,
both in Webster's Second) might be constructible. They discovered
that a list of single-word tautonyms was too small for this purpose,
so allowed hyphenated words and two-word phrases as well. Working from a list of only 350 tautonyms, they devised the square given
below:

```
R  A  B  B  I  R  A  B  B  I
A  S  A  I  L  A  S  A  I  L
B  A  S  S  A  B  A  S  S  A
B  I  S  O  N  B  I  S  O  N
I  L  A  N  G  I  L  A  N  G
R  A  B  B  I  R  A  B  B  I
A  S  A  I  L  A  S  A  I  L
B  A  S  S  A  B  A  S  S  A
B  I  S  O  N  B  I  S  O  N
I  L  A  N  G  I  L  A  N  G
```

Definitions and sources for the five words, listed alphabetically,
are given below.

A SAIL! A SAIL! -- Familiar Quotations by John Bartlett, 14th Edition,

Revised and Enlarged, published by Little, Brown and Company (Boston and Toronto, 1968) . The quotation including our tautonym is from The Rime of the Ancient Mariner by Samuel Taylor Coleridge, probably his greatest poetic work. The following lines appear in Part III, Stanza 4:

> I bit my arm, I sucked the blood,
> And cried, A sail! a sail!

BASSA-BASSA -- Notes for a Glossary of Words and Phrases of Barbadian Dialect by Frank A. Collymore, published by Advocate Company (Bridgetown, Barbados, 1970) . This glossary defines BASSA-BASSA as general confusion, noise, and, in some cases, exchange of blows. "Boy, when the spree over, we going make bassa-bassa." The origin of the word is obscure, possibly an importation from Trinidad. For those who might argue that the dialect of Barbados lies outside the pale of English, we must point out that Barbados, an island in the Lesser Antilles of the West Indies, was a British possession from 1605 to 1966, and is now a member of the (British) Commonwealth of Nations, in the same way as are Canada, Australia, New Zealand, and the United Kingdom itself. The 1973 Edition of The Official Associated Press Almanac calls Barbados "perhaps even more British than Britain". English is the official and universal language of the island.

BISON BISON -- The American Heritage Dictionary of the English Language edited by William Morris, published jointly by American Heritage Publishing Company, Inc., and Houghton Mifflin Company (Boston; New York; Atlanta; Geneva, Illionis; Dallas; Palo Alto, California, 1971) . BISON BISON is the scientific (genus + species) name for the bison, a hoofed animal of western North America (see definition of "bison") .

ILANG-ILANG -- The World Book Dictionary edited by Clarence L. Barnhart, a Thorndike-Barnhart Dictionary published exclusively for Field Enterprises Educational Corporation (Chicago, London, Rome, Stockholm, Sydney, Toronto, 1968) . This is a variant spelling of YLANG-YLANG, a tree native to the Phillippines, Java, and India, having fragrant, drooping, greenish-yellow flowers.

RABBI, RABBI -- The New Testament and the Book of Psalms, King James Version, published by the American Bible Society (New York, 1972) . In the Gospel According to Saint Matthew, Chapter 23, Verse 7 reads as follows:

> And greetings in the markets,
> and to be called of men, Rabbi, Rabbi.

(1) Of the words in the square, 60 % are recognizable at sight as being English
(2) The square employs five different words, each appearing twice horizontally and twice vertically

(3) All of the sources are works published within the past five years, making the square as current as is humanly possible
(4) The five words are taken from five different sources
(5) All five words are independent terms, as contrasted with a word that appears only as part of a two-word term
(6) Proper nouns have been excluded, and the square consists entirely of English words
(7) Instead of being exclusively hyphenated words, the terms display a pleasing variety of "internal" punctuation

On the other hand, the use of literary quotations for tautonyms is likely to be unacceptable to many logologists. A fully acceptable ten-by-ten word square is extremely unlikely to be found.

Cubism   (Jeff Grant)

In the February 1976 issue of Word Ways, Paul Remley presented an interesting article on three-dimensional word cubes of the sixth order. After re-reading this recently, I decided to attempt a solution using words taken from a single reference only. Mr. Remley stated that he was convinced such a solution existed, and was proved correct when the following cube presented itself after a number of hours delving into the Oxford English Dictionary:

```
1  R E M A D E      2  E N A M E L      3  M A C U L A
   E N A M E L         N A R I N E         A R E N A S
   M A C U L A         A R E N A S         C E R I T E
   A M U L E T         M I N I M E         U N I T E R
   D E L E T E         E N A M O R         L A T E R E
   E L A T E R         L E S E R E         A S E R E D

4  A M U L E T      5  D E L E T E      6  E L A T E R
   M I N I M E         E N A M O R         L E S E R E
   U N I T E R         L A T E R E         A S E R E D
   L I T O T E         E M E T I N         T E R E N E
   E M E T I N         T O R I E D         E R E N D E
   T E R E N E         E R E N D E         R E D E E M
```

If you take the letter in the top left corner of the first square (R), then add the corresponding letter in the second square (E), and so on down the line, you end up with the word REMADE, which is the first word on the first level. The same can be done starting from any other letter in the first square.

Encouraged by my early success, I resolved to have a go at the much more difficult problem of a 6 x 6 x 6 non-symmetrical cube, using 108 different words:

```
1 S C R A S H    2 C H I S T E    3 R A T T E L
  T R A N T E      R E S E E N      A P E R N E
  R A T T A R      A M A R N A      M O N I E R
  E N T E R D      P E R P E R      I D E O M E
  V I A G G E      E N C A L M      E A R L A P
  E A S S E L      S T O W S E      S L E E S S

4 E S T E R E    5 P T E R I S    6 S E R E S T
  V E R R E N      A R R E S T      T E E R T S
  O V A L L E      N A I L E R      A L D E R E
  R E D D E D      O L E I T Y      T E R C E T
  Y N A L F E      A E S S E N      T R E T S S
  E E S S E S      N E T H R E      E S S S S E
```

Of the 108 words used, 82 can be found in the Oxford English Diction-
ary (OED) , or inferred from words therein; 5 appear in Webster's
Third Edition (Web 3) ; and 4 in the English Dialect Dictionary (EDD)
There are 2 foreign words used, and 3 place-names from Webster's
New Geographical Dictionary (WNGD) .

The remaining 12 words are made up of inferred terms such as
REPERE (to 'pere' again, to reappear) and ANT-EGS (a reformed
spelling and probable early spelling of 'ant-eggs') , two-word terms
like HE MENT (dialectic form of 'he mended') , and citation forms
plural such as SWESH'S. I am sure that a perfect solution for the
6 x 6 x 6 non-symmetrical cube is possible, but it will undoubtedly
involve a lot of hard work, and probably a little luck, to discover it.

Despite failing to find a complete solution, I decided to progress
to the next level and attempt a symmetrical 7 x 7 x 7 cube. This also
proved to be an extremely difficult challenge:

```
1 P L U S S E D  2 L U N E T T E  3 U N G R E A T
  L U N E T T E    U R A L I U M    N A Y A N T E
  U N G R E A T    N A Y A N T E    G Y A N T E R
  S E R R I T A    E L A A T E R    R A N G A L E
  S T E I N I N    T I N T I L Y    E N T A B L E
  E T A T I S T    T U T E L L E    A T E L L A N
  D E T A N T S    E M E R Y E S    T E R E E N S

         4 S E R R I T A  5 S T E I N I N
           E L A A T E R    T I N T I L Y
           R A N G A L E    E N T A B L E
           R A G T I M E    I T A I L E S
           I T A I L E S    N I B L I C S
           T E L M E S T    I L L E C T E
           A R E E S T S    N Y E S S E S
```

```
6  E  T  A  T  I  S  T      7  D  E  T  A  N  T  S
   T  U  T  E  L  L  E         E  M  E  R  Y  E  S
   A  T  E  L  L  A  N         T  E  R  E  E  N  S
   T  E  L  M  E  S  T         A  R  E  E  S  T  S
   I  L  L  E  C  T  E         N  Y  E  S  S  E  S
   S  L  A  S  T  E  R         T  E  N  T  E  R  S
   T  E  N  T  E  R  S         S  S  S  S  S  S  S
```

Inferred or hard-to-locate terms are defined below:

AREESTS	an early spelling of 'arrests' (OED)
ELAATER	comparative form of 'elaat', an early form of 'elate' -- exalted, proud
EMERYES	plural of 'emerye', an early spelling of 'emery' (OED)
GYANTER	comparative form of 'gyant', an early form of 'giant' -- enormous, huge (OED)
ILLECTE	an early spelling of the verb 'illect' (to allure, entice) given in a 1534 OED quotation
NAYANTE	16th century spelling of 'naiant' (OED)
NIBLICS	variant of 'niblicks' in Webster's Second Edition
SERRITA	a town in Brazil, given in the Times Index-Gazetteer
SLASTER	variant of 'slaister' (OED)
SSSSSSS	the name of a movie, mentioned in the May 1978 Word Ways
STEININ'	slang or dialectic form of 'steining', variant of 'steening', the lining of a well
TELMEST	a town in Morocco, given in the Times Index-Gazetteer
TINTILY	the adverb that must logically be formed from 'tinty', full of tints
TUTELLE	the French word for 'protection', mentioned in the derivation of 'tutele' (OED)

ETATIST, PLUSSED and RAGTIME can be found in Webster's Third Edition, and the remaining words of the cube can be readily located in the Oxford English Dictionary.

HIGH-SCORING SCRABBLE

Since its introduction over a quarter-century ago, Scrabble has become the world's most popular word-oriented board game; in addition to English, there are French, German, Italian, Spanish and Russian versions on the market. Several books have been written on Scrabble strategy, and championship tournaments have been held annually in England and the United States.

For the logologist, however, Scrabble is less a game than a set of arbitrary rules converting words into numerical scores. He finds it possible to ask a number of theoretical questions about these scores, some easy to answer, others considerably more difficult.

The Best Word

In their book The Best (Farrar Straus & Giroux, 1974), Peter Passell and Leonard Ross claim that the highest-scoring seven-letter word that can be formed out of Scrabble tiles is JONQUIL (23 points), or, if a blank tile is allowed, QUIZ*ER (24 points). Not so! The words SQUEEZE (25 points) and QUIZ*ED (25 points) are so common that they can be found in boldface type in Webster's Pocket Dictionary; BEZIQUE (27 points) is only slightly more unusual. Ralph Beaman of Boothwyn, Pennsylvania believes that the highest-scoring word in boldface in Webster's Second or Third Unabridged is POPQUIZ (29 points). However, all of these are bettered by ZYXOMMA (30 points), the name of an Indian dragonfly in the Funk & Wagnalls Unabridged, noted by Josefa Byrne of Mill Valley, California in a letter to the New York Times (August 19, 1974). If Scrabble rules were relaxed to admit capitalized words, Ralph Beaman takes a giant step forward with QYRGHYZ (35 points), a variant spelling of Kirghiz found in boldface in Webster's Third. Of course, if some word could be formed out of the letters ZQJXKFY, the ultimate score of 49 could be achieved.

The Best Move

What is the highest score that can be achieved by a Scrabble player in one move? Joel D. Gaines of Honolulu, Hawaii may have been the first to investigate this question, devising a move scoring 1413 points in 1961. Unaware of this, Josefa Byrne arrived at a move of 1175 points, reported in Dmitri Borgmann's Beyond Language (Scribner's, 1967). In 1972 Darryl Francis of Hampton, Middlesex, England presented in Word Ways a single move of 1261 points.

All of these people quickly converged upon the optimum strategy: the completion of a fifteen-letter word along the edge of the board with seven letters, five of which are played in the first, fourth, eighth, twelfth and fifteenth positions. (The first, eighth and fifteenth fall on triple word squares, so that if all three are simultaneously filled the point value of the word is multiplied by 27; the fourth and twelfth triple the point count of any tile played on them.) In addition, it was recognized that the seven letters should also complete as many long words as possible (ideally, seven) running in the perpendicular direction to the fifteen-letter word. The rules of Scrabble impose further restrictions on the constructor, of course; the eight letters of the fifteen-letter word already in place must form a series of two-letter and three-letter words, and each perpendicular word has to form a word prior to the insertion of its initial or terminal letter.

Most of the points in the high-scoring move are contributed by the fifteen-letter word, suggesting that this should be selected first and the rest of the Scrabble array built around it. High-scoring letters are most valuable in the fourth and twelfth positions; ideally Q and Z, the only two 10-point letters, should be played there. Unfortunately, no such dictionary word is known, although such plausible coinages as JACQUARDERIZING and REEQUILIBRIZING have been suggested.

Reexamining the single move problem in the light of this theory, Darryl Francis searched Webster's Second and Third for high-scoring fifteen-letter words. Rejecting such 51-point specimens as PHENYL-HYDRAZINE, PREZYGAPOPHYSIS, DIAZOHYDROXIDES and PSYCH-OANALYZING, he pluralized BENZOXYCAMPHOR to obtain a 59-point word, and incorporated this into a single move of 1935 points, a substantial advance. The editors of the British magazine Games & Puzzles were so impressed by this achievement that they designed a year-long contest in 1973 around it: a price of 5 pounds sterling for the best solution received each month (if it bettered all previous months), and a 100 pound sterling award to the first person to exceed Darryl's score. (To add spice to the search, the contestants were not told what the target score was.) Starting with a score of 1700 reported in the February 1973 issue, the total edged slowly upwards: 1736 in May, 1751 in August, 1921 in September. The November 1973 issue reported that Ron Jerome of Bracknell, Berkshire, England independently discovered BENZOXYCAMPHORS and won the prize with a single-move score of 1945 points. The contest ended two months later with a 1949-point move. Later in 1974, Darryl Francis and Ron Jerome collaborated to raise the best single move to 1961 points. Jeff Grant's 1962-point solution is reproduced on the next page. Letters marked with an asterisk are represented by the two blank Scrabble tiles. The moves leading up to this were as follows:

1. er 2. squander 3. odd 4. oot 5. du, tue 6. tri, dut 7. squander-mania 8. im, fa, un, li, la, dutifull 9. elat 10. ex, ox 11. ta, amp 12. goyim 13. gaude 14. ie 15. in, en 16. odea 17. prover 18. aitts 19. es, eevn 20. vagabond 21. vagabondage 22. win 23. we, ie, leeds 24. floweret 25. tiew 26. io 27. ar, bi, oc, wink, ah, ga, rickshaw 28. an, gy, jinnyrickshaw 29. benzoxycamphors, proverb, gaudez, dutifully, squandermaniac, flowereth, vagabondager, jinnyrickshaws.

```
                     S                          J
                     Q                          I
                     U             E E V         N N
                     A   I T T     S     A       N Y
               O     N             G     A       R
               O     D D           F     B       R I
               T     U E           L     O       I C
       P       T     R I           O     O       C
       R   G O Y* I  M             W   I N       K
       O D*E A     F  A       L E E D            S
       V   U       U  N             R     A      H
       E   D       L  I             E     G      A
       R I E     E L  A T           T   I E      W
       B E N Z O X Y C A M P H O R S
```

The rules of the contest stipulated that allowable words had to appear in Webster's Second, Webster's Third, or the Oxford English Dictionary; plurals of nouns and inflected forms of verbs (-s, -ed, -ing) were also admitted. Proper names and hyphenated or apostrophized words were excluded. Several contestants discovered the 62-point word SESQUIOXIDIZING which yielded even higher one-move solutions; these, however, were disallowed on the grounds that the root word, SESQUIOXIDIZE, did not appear in any of these dictionaries (although the OED listed SESQUIOXIDIZED). Could the word be legitimatized by finding an example in chemical literature? Ralph Beaman, a chemist by profession, thought it doubtful, since the far commoner term OXIDIZING would be more likely to be used. The best solution using this word, a 2037-point one, was devised by Josefa Byrne:

```
S E S Q U I O X I D I Z I N G
J A   U P   R A T   B O T   A
A T   E E   N   D A O       S
M   E R N   T   S L*E E T   R
B E A R D   H       O       R
O   Y*E     P       G       O
K     D R I P       I F     N
I           H     A C E     O
N           Y E A R   W E M M
G           L       F       I
            L               C
            I               A
            T               L
            E               L
                            Y
```

1. hyll 2. year 3. phyllite 4. arf 5. ace 6. few 7. wem 8. mica
9. oologic, if 10. sleet 11. astronomical 12. astronomically
13. dao, as 14. bot, bas 15. it, in 16. anthophyllite 17. rat
18. it, id 19. io, or 20. drip 21. pended 22. beard 23. ea
24. uerry, up, ee, ern, ye 25. jambok 26. jamboking 27. ja, at,
at 28. eat, es 29. sesquioxidizing, querry, upended, xanthophyl-
lite, ibas, zoologic, gastronomically

The Best Game

The search for the best Scrabble game -- the highest combined score of both players -- is almost as old as the search for the best Scrabble move. It, too, was the subject of a Games & Puzzles contest (in 1974), but high scores were hampered by restricting contestants to a single dictionary, Chambers Twentieth Century. Using the three dictionaries allowed in the best-move contest, Ron Jerome achieved a score of 4047 points, but this in turn was bettered by Ralph Beaman with 4142:

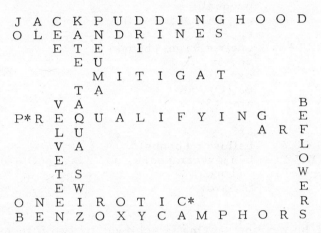

For the benefit of those who do not object to a 100-tile game, the remaining tile, an S, can be added to MITIGAT for 11 more points. All words in the solution follow the rules set down in the Games & Puzzles magazine two years ago for their highest-single-move contest; words not found in Webster's Second are labeled (3) if they are in Webster's Third, or (O) if they are in the Oxford English Dictionary. Starred letters indicate the use of blank tiles. The detailed moves are:

Score	Letters	Words Formed
114	AFILQUY	qualify (bonus)
27	GIN	qualifying
11	U	qu
12	A	qua
13	A	aqua
16	AT	taqua, ta
98	AGIIMTT	mitigat (O), ma (bonus)
5	U	uma (3)
7	EN	neuma
14	PU	pneuma, pu
2	A	an
85	DEILNOR	oleandrin, ud (O) (bonus)
3	I	ri
10	D	pud, dri (O)
10	AC	ac, al, ce

4	IN	in, in
17	E	oleandrine (O) , ne
19	GS	ing, gs, oleandrines (O)
1339	DDHJKOO	jackpuddinghood, jo, ka, di (bonus)
9	T	kat, te
16	E	cee, ete
20	E	kate, eu
10	EV	ve (3) , va
129	EEELNTV	velveteen, va, equalifying (O) , lu (bonus)
28	R	requalifying
84	*	prequalifying
12	IW	ew, wi (O) , ei (O)
2	E	en
74	INOORT*	oneirotic, ne (bonus)
20	OX	ro, ox, ox
18	Y	oxy, ty
5	AM	ca (O) , am
7	P	amp (3)
7	AR	ga, ar
6	F	arf
110	BEELORW	beflower (bonus)
1743	BCHORSZ	benzoxycamphors, ob, wiz, ic(O) , beflowers (bonus)
36	S	ts, swiz
4142		

Notice that the bulk of the scoring is achieved by two fifteen-letter
words along the edges of the board, much like the single-move strategy.   The difference between the two scores is even more remarkable when one realizes that Ron Jerome played all 100 tiles in his
game, but Ralph Beaman used only 99, arguing that a legal Scrabble
game must end when one player has no more tiles to play. (For a
100-tile game, add S to MITIGAT for 11 more points.)

Although no one has tried to construct a high-scoring game using
SESQUIOXIDIZING, Ralph Beaman has theorized that it might score
as much as 4260 points.

PLACE NAME WORDPLAY

Most logological investigations concentrate on dictionary words, shunning the much larger world of onomastics, or names. (For an appreciation of its scope, the reader is referred to Leslie Dunkling's The Guinness Book of Names, published by Guinness Superlatives in 1974.) The reasons for this are obscure, but may be related to the fact that dictionary nouns are abstractions which apply to many different objects, whereas names are merely labels for specific entities. Nevertheless, names are legitimate objects of logological inquiry; many, in fact, are more familiar to the average person than most dictionary words. This chapter focuses on a small part of the corpus of names: those which identify cities, towns and villages.

American Place Names   (Dmitri A. Borgmann)

For the purposes of this study, an American place name is the name of a community such as a city, town, township, village or hamlet. Included in the concept of a community are post offices and railroad stations upon which names have been conferred, whether or not they are populated. Excluded are all other place names, both those designating physical features and those designating other man-made features. Experience has shown that most people are more interested in community names than in the names of mountains, lakes and rivers.

Several aspects of these names must be defined: space, time and reference sources. American names are hereby decreed to be those included in the United States or in any territory that is a United States possession or commonwealth, or which have been included in the specified area at any past time, and which appear or have appeared in any reputable published reference work.

Each community name in the text that follows is identified by state or other location. Given in parentheses is the name of the county or parish or census division or other appropriate unit in which the community name is or was found, and a numeral identifying one reference work in which the name is included. A bibliography listing these reference works numerically is given at the end of this article.

The first and most obvious pair of questions that can be raised about American place names must be: (1) What is the shortest such name? (2) What is the longest such name? Simple as are the questions, the corresponding answers are surprisingly complex.

Taking up the problem of the shortest name first, we find that two-letter specimens are too common to merit notice, except for the fact that there is an astonishing concentration of them in the Commonwealth of Kentucky: ED (Casey-2) , EP (Owen-4) , EP (Pike-2) , EX (Grayson-3) , O.K. (Pulaski-1) , OZ (McCreary-1) , UZ (Letcher-1), and VI (Pike-2) . Consequently, our search focuses on one-letter names.

In West Virginia, we find a town named SIX (McDowell-5) . Here is a name that could be, and presumably sometimes has been, written "6", a one-character representation. However, a numeral is not a letter, so we continue searching. In Kentucky, we spot the town of ZERO (Hart-2) , which could be represented as "0". This character exhibits a dual aspect, since it is both a numeral and a letter. Still, it isn't the real thing, leaving us with a feeling of dissatisfaction.

In Michigan, we stumble on the genuine article: Y (Oscoda-3) . The town is in the extreme southeast corner of its county. Unfortunately, the town belongs to another era, for the only human habitation anywhere nearby in that county today is the Old Baldy Tower of the United States Forest Service. E, Maine (Aroostook-1) , another one-letter name, is somewhat questionable as it is PLANTATION OF E in full.

Although two-letter names are too common to be interesting, we must concede that names beginning with three consecutive two-letter words are a rarity. Two examples: PA PA ME, Michigan (Oceana-3) , and CE JA DE GALISTEO, New Mexico (San Miguel-3) .

With a relatively easy problem solved, we turn to the far more difficult problem of locating the longest name. Long names fall into three categories: those written as one solid word, those that are single but hyphenated words, and those consisting of two or more separate words.

In the first category, the name that leaps instantly to mind is that of a crossroads hamlet in Virginia, scene of a famous Civil War battle in May of 1863 resulting in the death of Stonewall Jackson: CHANCELLORSVILLE (Spottsylvania-6) . The anti-logological forces of history have not been kind to this 16-letter name. Research uncovers the sad fact that its name was subsequently changed to SCREAMERVILLE (5) , only 13 letters, and that it is known today simply as CHANCELLOR (1) , a mere 10 letters.

Persistent efforts succeed in replacing CHANCELLORSVILLE with a variety of other 16-letter names: CHICKASAWHATCHEE, Georgia (Terrell-1) , also spelled CHICHASAWHATCHIE (5) ; and numerous towns in Pennsylvania: McALLISTERSVILLE (Juniata-7) , McLAUGHLINSVILLE (Westmoreland-7) , MIDDLESMITHFIELD (Monroe-3) , PENNINGTONSVILLE (Chester-3) , and SOUTHAMPTONVILLE (Bucks-3) . Two others are BATCHELDERSVILLE, Illinois (Calhoun-18) and CHRISTIANSBURGH'S Depot, Virginia (Montgomery-3) , the first very long name that is the initial word of a compound name. Does the apostrophe destroy the " solidity" ? The challenge becomes to find 17-letter names.

Three have turned up: KLEINFELTERSVILLE, Pennsylvania (York-3), KLEINFELTERSVILLE, Pennsylvania (Lebanon-1), and MOOSELOOKMEGUNTIC, Maine (Franklin-1). Since various states boast towns named LIBERTYVILLE, there ought to be a 17-letter INDEPENDENCEVILLE somewhere, but it has not yet been found.

It seems impossible for 17 letters to represent the summit of American achievement. Our language permits entirely plausible one-word names of significantly greater length to be formed. A particularly meritorious example is the 25-letter concoction MacTHISTLE-THWAITESBOROUGH, derived from THISTLETHWAITE, Louisiana (St. Landry-1), adding the Scottish name prefix Mac- in recognition of the fact that the thistle is the national emblem of Scotland. Accordingly, the grim search for longer names has continued.

The key to success lies in taking a truly extended historical view of the problem. Once upon a time, somewhere in central New York, there was a Mohawk Indian village bearing the 25-letter name of KOWOGOCONNUGHARIEGUGHARIE (8). A casual examination of Hodge's monumental work will not locate this name, for it is buried in lightface type in a list of Mohawk villages included at the end of the article MOHAWK (see Volume 1, Page 924, Column 2).

It is a most curious thing. The 25-letter name is one of 14 Mohawk villages listed at the specified location. Each of the other 13 names, of little interest because much shorter, is also a boldface entry in its own right in Hodge's work. The 25-letter name is not, leaving us in the dark about its exact location and raising doubts about its authenticity. A typical logological mystery!

Next to be considered are one-word hyphenated names. Here the undoubted champion is the 22-letter CHARLESTON-ON-THE-KANAWHA, West Virginia (Kanawha-19), an old name of the state capital. Two good 18-letter examples are HASTINGS-UPON-HUDSON (Westchester-5) and ENGLEWOOD-ON-THE-HILL, Illinois (Cook-18).

Finally, we come to the multiple-word names. Here, a new refinement of our definition of American place names must be introduced. In recent years, large atlases such as Source 1 have inserted into their indexes all sorts of strange entities that violate the concept of a community, but have exceedingly long, compound names: railway junctions, veterans' hospitals, shopping centers, correctional institutions, naval stations, air force stations, and others. We decide to exclude all such entities from consideration in the course of our search.

Typical of a very long town name of the "genuine" sort is the following 34-letter name: THE ALEUT COMMUNITY OF SAINT PAUL ISLAND, Alaska (Aleutian Islands-1). The name can probably be surpassed in length, but only by a tedious and cumbersome search, picking one's way past scores of longer but unacceptable names.

We cannot let the matter rest on that basis, and a wide sweep of references follows. First to commend itself to our attention is one form of the original name of Los Angeles, California: EL PUEBLO DE NUESTRA SENORA LA REINA DE LOS ANGELES DE PORCIUN-CULA (Los Angeles-10). This name was bestowed on the community by the Spaniards in 1781 and remained in use, at least officially, until 1847.

While a 55-letter name is meritorious, it can be topped by some of the objectionable classes of names we are excluding. Consequently, an even longer name becomes imperative, and we continue our quest until a 69-letter specimen turns up: LA MISION DE NUESTRO SERAFICO PADRE SAN FRANCISCO DE ASIS A LA LAGUNA DE LOS DOLORES (San Francisco-11). This was the name of a presidio or fortified settlement established in 1776 in the San Francisco area. It was subsequently absorbed by the nearby village of Yerba Buena, which later changed its name to become the San Francisco of today. " The Mission of Our Seraphic Father Saint Francis of Assisi at the Lake of Our Lady of the Sorrows" has carried the day for us. Note that the English translation of the Spanish name is even longer -- 79 letters!

We turn our attention now to tautonymic place names. Although these are commonplace in some parts of the world -- so common that one may actually get tired of seeing them -- it is quite different in the United States, where considerable ingenuity must be invested in assembling them. Four-letter names, tautonymic though they may be, are too short to excite admiration in a professional logologist or onomatologist, and our search commences at the six-letter level.

Extended investigation brings only six names to light: PAW PAW, Michigan (Van Buren-1), YUM YUM, Tennessee (Fayette-1), ELE-ELE, Hawaii (Kauai-1), ILIILI, American Samoa (Tutuila-12), HUEHUE, Hawaii (Hawaii-1), and LOU LOU, Montana (Missoula-3). The latter is not to be confused with LO LO, Montana (Missoula-3), through the post office of which LOU LOU happens to receive its mail, even though the map in this atlas equates the two names. Two of these tautonyms are also palindromes, insuring them a permanent place in the Logological Hall of Fame.

Moving on to the eight-letter level, we find KUMUKUMU, Hawaii (Kauai-1), PAGO PAGO, the capital of American Samoa (Tutuila-12), SING SING, New York (Westchester-3), TOPA TOPA, California (Ventura-1), and LAHILAHI, Hawaii (Honolulu-4). In a typical display of anti-logological sentiment, the town of Sing Sing was renamed OSSINING in 1901.

Next is the ten-letter level, on which we are confronted by BADEN BADEN, Illinois (Bond-3), BICOL-BICOL, The Philippines (Luzon-13), and PANGOPANGO, an older form of the name PAGO PAGO (6). Shortening of PANGOPANGO to PAGO PAGO is yet another instance of the anti-logological currents swirling about us. For the benefit of

skeptics, we hasten to point out that BICOL-BICOL is taken from an
atlas published five years after The Philippines became a possession
of the United States. Finally, something reasonably familiar greets
us on the ten-level: WALLA WALLA, Washington (Walla Walla-1).
The new breed of Post Office abbreviations for our state names permits WALLA WALLA, WA. to join SENSUOUSNESS and LEVITATIVELY
as the only English twelve-letter anchored palindromes.

Can we be satisfied with ten-letter tautonyms? Of course not!
Longer ones must and will be found. Our first attempt to break
through to a higher level revolves around imperfect longer specimens.
Thus, we discover HETCH HETCHY, California (Tuolumne-3), from
which we would like to remove the final letter, as we also would like
to do in the case of KINNICKINNICK, Ohio (Ross-1). As for the compound designation EIGHTY EIGHT, KY. (Barren-1), deletion of the K
would create a twelve-letter tautonym. In the way of near misses, we
commend to your care the 14-letter specimen AUBBEENAUBBE, IN.
(Fulton-1). If only the I could be made an E!

The largest city in the Western Hemisphere shows us the way to
success. Who can deny that NEW YORK, NEW YORK is a fourteen-
letter tautonym? Using the same method, we quickly come across
ILLINOIS, ILLINOIS (Alexander-1) and WEST VIRGINIA, WEST VIR-
GINIA (Kanawha-4). The same technique can be extended to produce
the tautonymist's ultimate dream. Instead of combining city and state,
let us combine city, county, and state. That gives us OKLAHOMA,
OKLAHOMA, OKLAHOMA (Oklahoma-4), a 24-letter, three-part
tautonym! The atlas used was published in 1911. In 1923, the name
of the city was officially changed to OKLAHOMA CITY, yet another
instance of rampant anti-logology. The old name appeared as late as
1945, in the Funk & Wagnalls Unabridged Dictionary, but was cor-
rected by the time of the 1953 printing.

Palindromes, two examples of which have already been noted
briefly in connection with our review of tautonyms, are even more
difficult to find. From a population standpoint, the nation's largest
palindromic community appears to be ADA, Oklahoma (Pontotoc-1),
but the name uses only three letters, and a population of barely
15,000 is nothing to brag about, anyway.

More interesting to the onomatologist are names of seven or more
letters. These include KAYAYAK, Alaska (Bristol Bay-21), GLEN-
ELG, Maryland (Howard-1), NEW OWEN, Kentucky (Owen-14), and
OKONOKO, West Virginia (Hampshire-1). The first is less inspir-
ingly shown as KAGUYAK on the map in this atlas. The name NEW
OWEN is rather suspect because other atlases list it as NEW, OWEN
(1) -- that is, as a town named NEW in the county named OWEN.

Naturally, only four worthwhile palindromes do not suffice, and
a combination of techniques produces these further examples: OXO-
BOXO Lake, Connecticut (New London-1), a name we should like to
shorten to OXOBOXO; OMAHA, MO. (Putnam-1); APOLLO, PA.

(Armstrong-1); KANAKANAK, Alaska (Bristol Bay-15), and
ADAVEN, NEVADA (Nye-15). This twelve-letter palindromic
champion is the victim of the usual anti-logological activity; even
though it appears on the map in Source 16, it is not indexed in that
source, and has been suppressed entirely in Sources 1 and 14!

If the community of Sion, Texas (Walker-4) could be transplanted
to Illinois, the result would be another twelve-letter palindrome:
SION, ILLINOIS. What we actually have, unfortunately, is ZION,
ILLINOIS (Lake-1). With infinite regret, we note that the name of
a height in Jerusalem, a city currently completely under Israeli sov-
ereignty, may be written either as ZION or as SION. Not so ZION,
Illinois.

What are the strangest town names in America? No two individuals
are likely to agree on this subject. Our own three candidates are
TRUTH OR CONSEQUENCES, New Mexico (Sierra-1), renamed from
HOT SPRINGS in 1950, after a then-popular radio program (see Sources 6 and 10; its original Spanish name had been the 28-letter delight
LOS OJOS CALIENTES DE LOS PALOMAS, "Hot Springs of the
Doves" -- see Source 17); EWIGE QUAL, Illinois (Cook-18), now a
part of Glencoe but originally an independent community, the German
name of which means "Eternal Torture"; and WHO'D A THOUGHT IT,
Alabama (Jefferson-1), now a part of Birmingham. Readers are in-
vited to contribute equally strange names to our collection.

What name is written with the largest number of periods or full
stops? So far as we can determine, it is A.B.C., Tennessee (Sum-
ner-4), known to the railroads as TURNERS. Significantly, perhaps,
the community receives its mail through the post office in WEST-
MORELAND, Tennessee (Sumner-1)!

What name appears in the largest number of different states?
No intensive study of that problem has ever been undertaken. A pre-
liminary search through Source 1 has uncovered towns named WASH-
INGTON and SPRINGFIELD in 32 different states each (not counting
WASHINGTON, D.C., which is not in any state); towns named JACK-
SON in 33 different states; and towns named WARREN in 34 different
states. These figures could obviously be increased by adding towns
found only in older atlases and gazetteers, but there is the delicate
esthetic question as to whether that would be a proper thing to do.
Are there other names that occur more extensively in any one major
geographic reference work?

If all place names in the United States were arranged in one continuous alphabetical order, which name would be first, which would fall
at the precise midpoint, and which would be the very last one?

Using ordinary standards, the very first name is AABYE, Minnesota (Norman-3), located in the southwestern part of its county: a
fine Scandinavian name. Few logologists, of course, are ordinary

people, so ordinary standards do not satisfy. If we adopt the alphabetization principles followed by atlases such as those published by
C.S. Hammond and Company, then a name such as EL TORO precedes
ELBA instead of following it. This opens up new vistas, and we soon
discover AA JUNCTION, Arkansas (Johnson-14). Even this name,
however, is surpassed by A B C, Tennessee (Sumner-4). The three
letters comprising the name are written separately in Source 5, with
no periods between them, making alphabetization on the basis of the
first word being "A" mandatory. (However, purists may object to
the fact that the same reference also lists this town as A.B.C. --
see the previous article in this series.)

Starting with ordinary standards once more, the very last name is
ZYRZA, Georgia (Putnam-4), a community receiving its mail through
the county seat of Eatonton. If we broaden our perception of a community ever so slightly, however, we light upon ZZYZX SPRINGS, California (San Bernardino-23). ZZYZX SPRINGS is both a hydrologic feature and a privately owned spa catering to the senior citizen, about
8 1/2 miles south of Baker, on the western edge of Soda Dry Lake, off
the abandoned right-of-way of the old Tonopah and Tidewater Railroad.

Where is the midpoint of our alphabet? Between M and N. Consequently, it may be approached from either direction, but never
reached. Starting from the front of the alphabet, the name closest
to the midpoint is MYTON, Utah (Duchesne-1). Starting from the
back of the alphabet, the name closest to the midpoint is NAAHTEE,
Arizona (Navajo-24). Or is it? A little digging yields NAAGETL,
a Yurok Indian village on the lower Klamath river, just below AYO-
OTL and above the mouth of Blue creek, in northwestern California
(Source 8).

Up to this point, we have been considering names from a psycho-
logical standpoint: individually. Let us now consider them sociologi-
cally: in groups. Taken in groups, American place names exhibit
some remarkable characteristics. Suppose, for example, someone
were to ask you in what one state you might find LEWISTON, KOKOMO,
and RENTON. Would you guess at Idaho, or Indiana, or Washington?
If you did, you'd have to guess again, because the correct answer is
Hawaii (Source 1). Or, you might be asked to identify the one state
in which you could find CINCINNATI, CLEVELAND, and COLUMBUS.
Yes, all three are in Ohio, but all three are also in Arkansas (Source
1) and in Indiana (Source 1).

Do you recognize ATHENS, BELFAST, BELGRADE, LISBON,
MADRID, MOSCOW, PARIS, ROME, STOCKHOLM, and VIENNA as
European capitals? Are the names BREMEN, CALAIS, DRESDEN,
FRANKFORT, HANOVER, NAPLES, PALERMO, SORRENTO and
VERONA familiar to you as well-known cities in Germany, Italy, and
France? Have you been under the illusion that DENMARK, NORWAY,
POLAND, SCOTLAND, SWEDEN, and WALES are countries in Eur-
ope? Have you been ready to swear on a stack of Bibles that BRIS-

TOL, CAMBRIDGE, DOVER, LEEDS, MANCHESTER, MONMOUTH, NEWCASTLE, OXFORD, and PLYMOUTH are cities in England? Disabuse yourself of these fanciful notions. Taken as a group, all 34 names are those of towns in the state of Maine (Source 1).

You look at a map of one of our states, published today. On that map, you see town names such as SIKUL HIMATK, PIA OIK, KOXI-KUX, SIVILI CHUCHG, VAIVA VO, WAWK HUDUNIK, SCHUCHK, GU VO, MISHONGNOVI, TAT MOMOLI, TEEC NES POS, VAINOM KUG, and CHUI CHUISCHU. Where are you? In Arizona, of course (Source 1) -- those are present-day Indian villages, mostly Papago and Navajo.

BIBLIOGRAPHY

1. 1972 Commercial Atlas & Marketing Guide, 103rd Edition, Rand McNally & Company, Chicago, New York, and San Francisco, 1972.
2. Rand McNally Pocket Maps of Kentucky, Rand McNally & Company, Chicago, New York, and San Francisco, 1934.
3. Rand, McNally & Co.'s Enlarged Business Atlas and Shippers' Guide, 23rd Edition, Rand, McNally & Company, Chicago, 1893.
4. Rand McNally & Co.'s Commercial Atlas of America, 1st Edition, Rand McNally & Company, Chicago, 1911.
5. Rand McNally World Atlas, Premier Edition, Rand McNally & Company, New York, Chicago, and San Francisco, 1927.
6. Webster's Geographical Dictionary, Revised Edition, G. & C. Merriam Company, Springfield, Massachusetts, 1963.
7. A New and Complete Gazetteer of the United States, by Thomas Baldwin and J. Thomas, Lippincott, Grambo & Co., Philadelphia, 1854.
8. Handbook of American Indians North of Mexico, by Frederick Webb Hodge, Rowman and Littlefield, Inc., New York, 1965.
9. The New Merriam-Webster Pocket Dictionary, A Pocket Cardinal Edition, Pocket Books, Inc., New York, 1964 and 1970 Editions only.
10. The New Century Cyclopedia of Names, edited by Clarence L. Barnhart, Appleton-Century-Crofts, Inc., New York, 1954.
11. California Place Names, by Erwin G. Gudde, Revised and Enlarged Edition, University of California Press, Berkeley and Los Angeles, 1960.
12. The National Geographic Map of the Pacific Ocean, Inset Map No. 28 (Tutuila, Eastern Samoa), published with the December, 1952 issue of The National Geographic Magazine, Washington, 1952.
13. Rand McNally & Co.'s Indexed Atlas of the World, Volume II (Foreign Countries), Rand, McNally & Company, Chicago, New York, London, and Berlin, 1903.
14. Rand McNally Commercial Atlas and Marketing Guide, 95th Edition, Rand McNally & Company, New York, Chicago, and San Francisco, 1964.

15. Rand McNally Cosmopolitan World Atlas, Rand McNally & Company, Chicago, New York, and San Francisco, 1951.
16. Rand McNally Road Atlas, United States/Canada/Mexico, 49th Annual Edition, Rand McNally & Company, Chicago, New York, and San Francisco, 1973.
17. The Encyclopedia Americana, International Edition, Americana Corporation, New York, 1970 (Volume 27).
18. Illinois Place Names, by James N. Adams, Occasional Publications Number 54, Illinois State Historical Society, Springfield, Illinois, 1968.
19. West Virginia Place Names, by Hamill Kenny, The Place Name Press, Piedmont, West Virginia, 1945.
20. A Literary & Historical Atlas of America, by J. G. Bartholomew, Revised by Samuel McKee, Jr., Everyman's Library Volume No. 553, J. M. Dent & Sons, London & Toronto, 1930.
21. The Century Atlas of the World, prepared under the superintendence of Benjamin E. Smith, The Century Company, New York, 1902.
22. Sixth Report of the United States Geographic Board, 1890 to 1932, United States Government Printing Office, Washington, 1933.
23. San Bernardino County, an undated map published by Automobile Club of Southern California, Los Angeles, prior to 1965.
24. The Times Index-Gazetteer of the World, The Times Publishing Company, London, 1965.

A State Name Chain   (Darryl H. Francis)

Often, while searching through atlases and gazetteers of the United States, we have been surprised at the number of communities which possess names identical with various states. For example, there is a town called OREGON in Holt County, Missouri, and there is a MAINE in Davie County, North Carolina. We felt that here was a logological phenomenon worth investigating further. So, we turned to the 1967 edition of the Rand McNally Commercial Atlas and Marketing Guide. This is a listing of about 115,000 place names the length and breadth of the United States. A complete examination of this work revealed just over two hundred instances of a community bearing the same name as one of the fifty states. Omitted from our list were variant spellings such as ARKANSAW or multi-word names such as IDAHO SPRINGS or ILLINOIS CAMP.

Not surprisingly, the most frequent community name on our list was WASHINGTON. But the two runners-up, WYOMING and DELA-WARE, did seem somewhat unexpected.

It was Dmitri Borgmann's idea that we use the list to construct a statename chain. In a statename chain, one attempts to construct a chain as long as possible reading: community A is in state B, community B is in state C, community C is in state D, and so on. The upper limit to such a chain is 50 links, corresponding to the fifty states; in reality, though, this figure cannot be closely approached. This derives from difficulties in finding communities with names such as NEW JERSEY, NEW MEXICO, NORTH DAKOTA and SOUTH CAROLINA. Even so, the fact that we found a NEW HAMPSHIRE (in Auglaize County, Ohio) and a WEST VIRGINIA (in St. Louis County, Minnesota) does not mean that NEW JERSEY, etc. cannot be found.

The pool of two hundred names was augmented by additional ones taken from the Century Atlas, plus several sent by Dmitri Borgmann from obscure atlases. This resulted in the following 26-link chain:

WYOMING is in Kent County, DELAWARE
DELAWARE is in Southampton County, VIRGINIA
VIRGINIA is in Kitsap County, WASHINGTON
WASHINGTON is in Knox County, MAINE
MAINE is in Coconino County, ARIZONA
ARIZONA is in Burt County, NEBRASKA
NEBRASKA is in Jennings County, INDIANA
INDIANA is in Indiana County, PENNSYLVANIA
PENNSYLVANIA is in Mobile County, ALABAMA
ALABAMA is in Genesee County, NEW YORK
NEW YORK is in Santa Rosa County, FLORIDA
FLORIDA is in Houghton County, MICHIGAN
MICHIGAN is in Osage County, KANSAS
KANSAS is in Seneca County, OHIO
OHIO is in Gunnison County, COLORADO

COLORADO is in South Central District, ALASKA
ALASKA is in Mineral County, WEST VIRGINIA
WEST VIRGINIA is in St. Louis County, MINNESOTA
MINNESOTA is in Colquitt County, GEORGIA
GEORGIA is in Lamar County, TEXAS
TEXAS is in Baltimore County, MARYLAND
MARYLAND is in East Baton Rouge County, LOUISIANA
LOUISIANA is in Pike County, MISSOURI
MISSOURI is in Brown County, ILLINOIS
ILLINOIS is in Sequoyah County, OKLAHOMA
OKLAHOMA is in Daviess County, KENTUCKY

State Name Charades

A charade sentence conceals words or phrases in its text. For
example, the following sentence, taken from the monthly journal published by Mensa, incorporates the numbers from one through nine in
order:

> Want a wooden overcoat? Buy Honest John Whitworth's health-
> reenergizing sulfo-uranyl-impregnated "Comfi-Vest" with its
> unique quasi-xyloid fibers -- obtainable only from the Paradise
> Vending Company, Harpursville Heights, Nineveh, New York.

In Problem 130 of Beyond Language (Scribner's, 1967), Dmitri
Borgmann suggested that charade sentences incorporating the name of
a state and its capital might serve a mnemonic to associate the two.
The following list of 50 mnemonics has been selected from his original
collection of 18, plus additions proposed by Charles E. Karrick of Tal-
lahassee, Florida, Mary Hazard of Rochester, New York, Murray
Pearce of Bismarck, North Dakota, Chester Karwoski of New Britain,
Connecticut, Leslie Card of Urbana, Illinois, Ernest Theimer of Rum-
son, New Jersey, and Josefa Byrne of Mill Valley, California.

A LAB AMAlgam was prepared in MONTGOMERYshire County, Wales.
AL, ASK Anne and JUNE A Useful question!
OmAR, I ZONAted the property with a PHOENIX-shaped tool.
O hARK, ANSA-Shaped vases may be shattered by LITTLE ROCKs!
Don't paniC, ALI, FOR NIAgara Falls enhances the SACRAMENT
    Of matrimony.

COLOR A DOll, hoyDEN, VERy neatly and quietly.
To disCONNECT, I CUT cables marked on a cHART FOR Destruction.
Schools which maDE LAW A REquired course DO VERy well.
FLORID Atheists treaT ALLAH, AS SEEn by Muslims, as non-
    existent.
Use an insectifuGE OR GIAnt insects will destroy thAT LANTAna
    field.

Do tHAW AI Immediately for supper, HON -- O, LULU, are you
    listening?

Are you afraID A HOstile hoBO IS Entering your house?

"He's ILL!", I NOISe about each SPRING, FIELDing comebacks
deftly.

IN DIANA's shop, I saw thIN DIANA POLIShing furniture.

RadIO WAves are dangerous, chiDES MO, IN ESsence.

PeKANS ASsimilate much, but are too wise to TOPE KAlsomine.

KEN, TUCK Your shirt in and be FRANK, FORThright and coura-
geous.

LOUIS, IAN And Eric BAT ON ROUGE-colored playing fields.

The MAIN Evil of the AUGUSTAn age was imperialism.

Did MARY LAND as ANNA POLIShed apples?

You can't sing at MASS? ACH, USE T. T. SlurBO'S TONsil spray.

During the epideMIC, HI, GANgrene overcame AlLAN'S INGrained
fear of doctors.

Be calM, INNES, OTAlgia won't arreST PAULA's hearing.

MISS, IS SIPPIng pink lemonade better than eating flapJACKS ON
the double?

MISS, OUR Index card, "Thomas JEFFERSON, CITY boy" is wrong.

GuM ON TAN Apparel irritates RacHEL, ENAbling her to rant.

Even if you wear fiNE BRAS, KAte, you won't look LINCOLNesque.

CaN EVA DAnce outside, with CARS ON CITY streets?

I kNEW HAMP'S HIREEling would great the deaCON CORDially.

She bought a NEW JERSEY when she couldn'T RENT ONe.

ReNEW MEXICO's wild pheaSANT, A FEral bird.

SiNEWY OR Knotted branches are typicAL BANYan tree characteristics.

When sparrows up NORTH CAROL INAnely, upsetting moRALE, I
GHoom them.

To the NORTH, DAKOTA red men were scalping rabBIS, MARC
Knew.

OH, I Only saw MexiCO, LUM; BUS was late.

By the broOK, LAHOMA, by the broOK, LAHOMA, CITYward we go.

At the zoo, I fOREGO Nothing as interesting aS A LEMur.

PENN, SYLVAN IAmbic poet, writes of HARRIS, BURGlar of jewels.

By sacrificing without myrRH, ODE, I SLANDer PROVIDENCE.

In the SOUTH, CAROL, INAction dates from pre-COLUMBIAN times.

Farther SOUTH, DAKOTA red men found a raPIER, REd with blood.

OfTEN, NESS EEls burn to browN ASH, VILLEin complains.

I mighT EXASperate my beAU, STINgy as I am.

Beware the rUT AHead of the SALT LAKE, CITY slicker!

A cleVER MONTage maker is SiMON T. PELIER.

As a VIRGIN, I Allure the RICH MONDays and all other days.

WASHING TONs of laundry requires OLYMPIAn powers.

You must go WEST, VIRGINIA, said CHARLES TONight.

LeWIS CONS INdians into believing that a noMAD IS ON duty.

The HebreW " YOM", INGa, doesn't mean aCHE, YEN, NEed or
desire for religion.

Piddletrenthide (Darryl H. Francis)

The London Times devotes a regular column to the reassignments of Church of England clerics. Buried among the announcements of August 21, 1974 was the following:

Diocese of Salisbury. The Rev J.E.B. Cattell, Vicar of Piddle-trenthide with Alton Pancras and Plush, to be priest-in-charge of Buckhorn Weston and Kington Magna.

This simple notice resulted in a flood of letters from readers during the next fortnight, many commenting on other strange British place-names. Here is a sampling, for the delectation of Word Ways readers:

Sir, There can surely never have been a more musical-sounding appointment in The Times than that of August 21, announcing that the vicar of Piddletrenthide with Alton Pancras and Plush is to be priest-in-charge of Buckhorn Weston and Kington Magna. Is there really a parish of Piddletrenthide with Alton Pancras and Plush? If so, I will have to retire there; it certainly is an improvement on "Maidstone". In 30 years' time, however, when I am ready to retire, that parish, too, will probably have a post-code, and it will merely be known as "Pwapap", for short.   P. H. H. Moore

Sir, When, some years ago I was down in that part of the world I saw a signpost which, on one of its arms, read: Plush, Folly, Mappowder, Piddletrenthide.   Simon Borrett

Sir, Mr Moore enquires in your issue of August 24 whether there really is such a place as Piddletrenthide. Yes, Mr Moore, there is; it's in West Dorset and is as delightful as its name implies. We also have Toller Pocorum, Sydling St Nicholas, Whitchurch Canonicorum, and Ryme Intrinseca, to name but four others. Can anywhere in the country match this area for the haunting quality of its village names? Trevor Jones

Sir, Mr Trevor Jones (Letters, August 30) has only to cross the border into Somerset to find village names just as evocative as those in Dorset. Wyke Champflower, Chilton Cantelo, Huish Episcopi, and Upton Noble are all within a few miles of my own village. Digby Meller

Sir, We read about Soho, Piccadilly, Petty France and Bedlam. Can you assure me that there really are such places in London? R. Belgrave, West Lodge, Piddlehinton, Dorset

Sir, Mr Moore's choice of parish for retirement is indeed difficult to fault (Piddletrenthide with Alton Pancras and Plush), but for sheer pleasure to the ear the redeployment of ecclesiastical strength in Yorkshire which appeared in your columns some 14 years ago remains supreme: "the Rev G. D. Beaglehole, Vicar of Kexby with Wilberfoss to be Vicar of Bossall with Buttercrambe". Aidan Reynolds

Sir, I have looked in vain for any mention of Sixpenny Handley (6d Handley) in Dorset in your correspondence columns. Are we to assume that it is now 2 1/2 p Handley?   Annys, Mother Superior, Convent of St John Baptist

Sir, For sheer deployment of ecclesiastical strength as well as for aural harmony Yorkshire can do even better than Mr Reynolds is prepared to allow, for in 1960 you also announced: " The Rev G. Christie, Rector of Roos with Tunstall-in-Holderness, Vicar of Garton with Grimston and Hilston and Rural Dean of South Holderness to be Vicar of Pocklington with Yapham-cum-Meltonby and Owsthorpe with Kilnwick Percy, and Millington with Great Givendale, and Rural Dean of Pocklington." It is understandably with regret that I sign myself as Michael Peel, Rector of Iver Heath (only).

Sir, We in Hampshire can surely beat them all with our three hearty Wallops -- Over, Middle and Nether.   A. Murray

Sir, One signpost in Shropshire reads simply: Homer 1, Wigwig 2. How's that for brevity and wit?   Anna A. M. Wells

Sir, I have greatly enjoyed this correspondence. I respectfully submit my own personal contribution. Gonville Aubie Ffrench-Beytagh, Rector of the United Parishes of Saint Vedast alias Foster with St Michael-le-Querne and St Matthew, Friday Street with St Peter, Cheap; St Alban, Wood Street with St Olave, Silver Street, St Michael, Wood Street and St Mary Staining; St Lawrence Jewry with St Mary Magdalene, Milk Street and St Michael Bassishaw; and St Anne & St Agnes, Gresham Street with St John Zachary, Gresham Street; and St Mary Aldermanbury

Sir, My current favourite in this class for any country is the eructative name of a station on the railway line from Brussels to Louvain: Erps-Kwerps.   Margaret Barclay

Sir, A few miles to the East of Oxford on the A40 a signpost points to " The Baldons". This simple omnibus name conceals the identities of Great Baldon, Little Baldon, Baldon in-between, Marsh Baldon, Toot Baldon, Baldon-on-the-Green, and Baldon. John H. Edmonds

Sir, May I on behalf of Scotland offer a brief contribution to this correspondence and draw attention to the tiny but ancient fishing village on the south shore of the Firth of Forth, which proudly bears the name " Society"?   Maurice Lyell, Puddephat's Farm

Sir, the first place listed in Part Two of the 1961 Census Index of Place Names aptly describes the efforts of your readers in this silly correspondence: Labour-in-vain. M. R. Huxley

<u>English Place Names</u>   (Darryl H. Francis)

Actually, the readers of the London Times have only hinted at the wealth of curious British place names.

We have assembled a list of 50 names, two for each letter of the alphabet (except X, for which no British placename seems to exist). All names in this list can be found in Bartholomew's Gazetteer of the British Isles, published by John Bartholomew, London and Edinburgh, 9th edition with supplement, 1966. The names here are of places, villages, towns, localities and parishes; names of rivers, hills, mountains, lakes, woods and other geographical features have been excluded.

Ampney Crucis	Ashby St. Ledgers
Barton-in-the-Beans	Burstwick cum Skeckling
Cadoxton-juxta-Neath	Cow Honeybourne
Deaf Hill cum Langdale	Dollar
Edenordinary	Even Swindon
Fighting Cocks	Freezywater
Germansweek	Great and Little Cowdens
Hanging Walls of Mark Anthony	Hereford St. John the Baptist
Indian Queens	Irlams o' the Height
Jericho	Jerusalem
Kill St. Nicholas	Knotty Ash
Leighton Buzzard	London Apprentice
Market Jew	Middle Wallop
Near Oxenhope	Norton sub Hamdon
Over Peover	O Wood Row
Pennycumquick	Peterston super Montem
Queen Camel	Quex
Readymoney	Rotten Row
Shoulder of Mutton Green	Stamford Baron St. Martin Without
Tolleshunt Knights	Top o' th' Hill
Up Ottery	Upperup
Ventongimps	Victoria Cross
Wendens Ambo	Westward Ho!
Yate and Pickup Bank	Yatton Keynell
Zeal Monachorum	Zouch Mills

BRITISH WORD PUZZLES

Modern-day logology has arisen from the confluence of three streams of activity -- academic linguistics, literary experimentation with constrictive forms, and word puzzling. Of these, the third is by far the most significant. This chapter examines a small but important part of word puzzling history -- the flowering of British puzzles during the eighteenth and nineteenth centuries. Although American word puzzles also developed during this period, they owe much to the British models which, in general, were developed earlier and were in some cases of very high literary quality.

Puzzles of the sort discussed below are rarely seen by the contemporary American; an occasional one is found in the Old Farmer's Almanac and similar publications. (A wide sampling of their puzzles from 1850 to 1975 can be found in The Old Farmer's Almanac Book of Old-Fashioned Puzzles, published by Yankee, Inc. at Dublin, N.H. in 1976.)

During the period surveyed in this chapter, puzzles ordinarily appeared in newspapers, magazines or books, and were solved by their readers working in isolation from other puzzlers. In the latter part of the nineteenth century, however, a number of puzzle clubs, mostly short-lived, were formed in various American cities; here members met and posed puzzles for each other to solve. The most long-lived of these organizations was the Eastern Puzzlers' League, which was formed at Pythagoras Hall in New York City on July 4, 1883, and survives today in metamorphosed form as the National Puzzlers' League. Its members still meet occasionally in conventions, but most of their puzzleistic activity is carried on in the pages of their monthly newsletter, The Enigma, to which members contribute original puzzles of the types depicted in this chapter.

Eighteenth-Century Puzzles   (William F. Shortz)

A rebirth of popularity in enigmas and word-play occurred in
Europe during the Renaissance period. During the sixteenth and
seventeenth centuries, numerous collections of riddles and word puzzles were published, including Demaundes Joyous (1511), A Little
Book of Riddles (1540), The Booke of Merry Riddles (prior to 1575,
and mentioned in Shakespeare's The Merry Wives of Windsor), Wit's
Academy (1656), and many others. Men of all walks of life riddled
and puzzled during idle hours.

Even by the beginning of the eighteenth century, however, very
few types of puzzles were in existence. Most popular were riddles
and enigmas, which men had been making and solving since antiquity.
Anagramming had come into vogue during the 1600s, and the making
of acrostics had been practiced for many years. But besides these
elementary puzzle forms, almost no other types were known.

A popular London magazine of the early 1700s, entitled Delights
for the Ingenious, or, A Monthly Entertainment for the Curious, contained an extensive puzzle department in each issue. The enigmas and
word-games that were printed in the magazine provide us with valuable
insights into word-puzzling of the period. Indeed, the February 1711
issue of Delights for the Ingenious presented an article on all of the
forms of word-play in vogue at the time.

Most frequently found in the magazine's puzzle department, almost to the exclusion of all other types of puzzles, were the enigmas.
William Walsh defines an enigma as "a description, perfectly true
in itself, but so ingeniously couched in metaphorical language that
the sense is not obvious, so that when put in the form of a question
it shall stimulate the curiosity and yet baffle the would-be interpret-
er"(William S. Walsh, Handy-Book of Literary Curiosities, Philadelphia, J.P. Lippincott Co., 1892, p. 293). The editor of Delights
for the Ingenious wrote in one issue, "A well-penn'd Enigma, art-
fully contriv'd, where-in Truth walks in Masquerade, and where a
Delicacy of Thought and Beauty of Expression shines throughout, is
one of the most agreeable and delightful entertainments that I know
of; and no less pleasant is the Explication, when it falls into the
Hands of an ingenious Answerer" (Delights for the Ingenious I, January 1711, p. 25).

An example of an enigma of the period is the following:

> "I'm thick, I'm thin, I'm short and long,
> And lov'd alike by Old and Young;
> I make Diseases, and I heal,
> And know what I shall ne'er reveal.
> The fairest Virgin, fraught with Pride,
> No Beauty from my View can hide.
> I rack the Miser, cure the Sot,
> And make, and oft detect a Plot:
> No lover that would happy be,
> Desires his Mistress more than me:
> Yet tho' a Thousand Charms I have,
> Next step from me is to the Grave."

And its explication, also in verse:

> "A Bed may be little or great, short or long,
> The Strong it makes weak, and the Weak it makes strong;
> Opprest with his Load, the Sot there finds Relief,
> And the Miser is rackt with the Fears of a Thief:
> The Lady's there gentle, and free to her Lover,
> And what might it not, cou'd it tell us, discover!
> There Plots are oft hatch'd, and as often detected,
> And things well contriv'd that are never effected:
> There dreaming of Peril and Pleasure we lie,
> Are wretched and happy, we are born and we die."
> (Delights for the Ingenious I, January 1711, p. 25)

Most enigmas, such as the previous one and the one which follows, rely on the paradoxes in the nature of their subjects to arouse the curiosity of the reader. This enigma is another good example from the early 1700s:

> "In young and old I do excite
> Painful Sensations, and Delight.
> All Men me as their Servant prize;
> But when I rule, I tyrannize:
> I can be seen, and heard, and smelt,
> Yea, more, I'm at a distance felt,
> I'm never bought nor sold; but yet,
> I am maintain'd with Charges great.
> There's but one Death in Nature found
> For me, and that is to be drown'd."
> (Delights for the Ingenious I, July-August-September
> 1711, p. 266)

The answer, of course, is "fire".

Most other word-play of the early 1700s was not designed to puzzle the reader, but simply to entertain him. Some of these forms of word-play, however, were later developed into types of puzzles. Examples include acrostics, anagrams, echo verses, and chronosticks. One recreational form known at the beginning of the eighteenth century appears to be the forerunner of the charade. The fact that it appeared as early as 1711 is very interesting, in view of what Isaac D'Israeli, an authority on the subject, wrote 170 years later: "The charade is of recent birth, and I cannot discover the origin of this species of logogriphes. It was not known in France so late as in 1771" (Isaac D'Israeli, Curiosities of Literature, Volume 1, New York, A. C. Armstrong and Son, 1881, p. 389).

The origin of the term "charade" itself is an enigma. Some people attribute it to the inventor of the puzzle. Others believe that it comes from the Spanish word charrada, meaning "speech of a clown". Still others are convinced that it comes from the Italian word schiarare, meaning "to disentangle" or "to clear up". The word "charade" did not come into usage until the 1770s and 1780s, but the puzzles were known quite a few years earlier. The February 1711 issue of Delights for the Ingenious contained the following "rebus":

> "From the Mate of the Cock, Winter-Corn in the Ground,
> The Christian Name of my Friend may be found:
> Join the song of a cat, to the Place Hermits dwell in,
> Gives the Sirname of him who does Musick excell in."

It was explained as follows: "Here the Mate of a Cock is a Hen: The Winter-Corn is either Wheat or Ry; but because it is to make up a Name, it is the latter that is meant: so the Christian Name is Henry. Then the Song of a Cat is what we call the Pur of a Cat; and the Place a Hermit dwells in is call'd a Cell: so the sirname is Purcell: So that this Rebus is upon the Name of M. HENRY PURCELL, the late famous Master of Musick, perhaps the best that ever England bred" (Delights for the Ingenious I, February 1711, p. 69).

During the 1700s, word puzzles appeared in books, magazines, and almanacs of all kinds. Even the highest-class literary journals printed occasional enigmas, acrostics, and miscellaneous puzzles. Such magazines included Town and Country Magazine, Gentleman's Magazine, the Agreeable Companion, and The Universal Magazine of Knowledge and Pleasure.

Perhaps the leading magazine which carried recreational verse was the London Magazine, which printed three to eight puzzles per year. The puzzles were evidently quite popular, as many solutions in verse were contributed by readers.

The following successive beheadment, with enigmatic qualities, was written by "Philocrupticus" and printed in the October 1748 number of the London Magazine:

> "Not like the diamond and gold,
> Which some few happy countries hold,
> In ev'ry clime more common I
> With stones and sand promiscuous lie: ...
> So chang'd I am, since rais'd from earth,
> That strangers could not guess my birth.
> My frame is delicate and nice,

But may be alter'd in a trice.
With gentle usage and fair wearing,
I last for years without repairing.
The sciences I much promote,
And truths discover of great note:
Astronomy and opticks too
Would, but for me, have little new. ...
My foremost letter set aside,
Leaves <u>one</u> that longs to be a bride;
And if <u>you</u> can the pretty maid
Her letter first to drop persuade,
You'll find, with pleasure, after all,
A meek and harmless <u>animal</u>."
(London Magazine XVII, October 1748, p. 471)

The solution is "glass-lass-ass".

Acrostics were also popular during the 1700s. Quite often the puzzles were based upon ladies' names, as this acrostic from a 1762 issue of London Magazine illustrates:

"A place of confinement, as dark as the night;
What's us'd as a token when persons unite;
That part of the day, when the sun disappears,
And leaves us surrounded with numerous fears;
What the heart ne'er enjoys when the mind's void of rest;
A word often us'd to deny a request.
These initials, when properly placed, you'll find,
The name of a damsel, that's constant and kind;
With modesty grac'd, and with beauty adorn'd;
With wisdom endu'd, and to virtue conform'd."
(London Magazine XXXI, November 1762, p. 619)

The five words reading across are "Grave", "Ring", "Evening", "Ease" and "No", and the initial letters, which form the acrostic, spell Miss GREEN.

Rudimentary charades appeared in the London Magazine as early as 1749. For many years the puzzles were based solely on the names of men and women or the names of places. The very crude example which follows was published in November 1750:

"The serum of milk, and where Noah's ark rested
Denotes a fair lady for virtue respected."
(London Magazine XIX, November 1750, p. 520)

The solution was printed in the next month's issue:

"The serum of milk must be -- <u>Whey</u>,
In obedience to God's command
The waters were drained away,
And Noah's ark rested on -- <u>Land</u>."
(London Magazine XIX, December 1750, p. 567)

This charade, printed in the year 1752, is based on the town of
Portsmouth:

> " To places where ships are safe from a storm
>   Add that which makes part of your face;
> And when these two are together, they'll form
>   The name of a very brave place. "
>   (London Magazine XXI, February 1752, p. 86)

Along with the magazines and almanacs which printed puzzles,
quite a few books were published containing enigmas and riddles,
both new and old. A few titles are these: Thesaurus Aenigmaticus;
or, A Collection of the most ingenious and diverting Aenigmas or
Riddles (1725), The Puzzle; being a choice collection of Conundrums (1745), The Edge Taken Off, or the conundrums and home-
clinches of the whetstone unriddled (1745), Youthful Amusements
in Verse (1757), and The Young Lady and Gentleman's New Riddle
Book (1794), among many others.

As can be seen from the titles above, puzzles were popular with
the common folk of England during the eighteenth century. Puzzles
were also very popular, however, with the intellectuals of the period.
Numerous writers, poets, and statesmen, noted for their more serious works, made and solved enigmas for their own entertainment.

Jonathan Swift (1667-1745), author of Gulliver's Travels, was
not averse to writing enigmas for amusement. He wrote in his Works
that, around 1724, " some ingenious gentlemen, friends to the author,
used to entertain themselves with writing riddles, and send them to
him and their other acquaintance; copies of which ran about, and
some of them were printed, both here (Dublin) and in England. The
author, at his leisure hours, fell into the same amusement; although
it be said that he thought them of no great merit, entertainment, or
use. However, by the advice of some persons, for whom the author
hath a great esteem, and who were pleased to send us the copies,
we have ventured to print the few following, as we have done two or
three before, and which are allowed to be genuine: Because we are
informed that several good judges have a taste for such kind of compositions" (Walter Scott, The Works of Jonathan Swift, D.D., Volume XV, Edinburgh, Archibald Constable and Co., 1814, p. 3).

The first enigma, a very clever one, was written by one of Dr.
Swift's friends:

> " Because I am by nature blind,
>   I wisely choose to walk behind;
> However, to avoid disgrace,
>   I let no creature see my face.
> My words are few, but spoke with sense;
>   And yet my speaking gives offence:
> Or if to whisper I presume
>   The company will fly the room.
> By all the world I am opprest:

> And my oppression gives them rest ..."
>   (The Works of Jonathan Swift, D.D., Volume XV, p. 9)

The solution is "the posteriors".

This second enigma was written by Dr. Swift himself, and was originally communicated to Oldisworth, who published it in the Muse's Mercury:

> "From India's burning clime I'm brought,
>   With cooling gales like zephyrs fraught.
>   Not Iris, when she paints the sky,
>   Can show more different hues than I;
>   Nor can she change her form so fast,
>   I'm now a sail, and now a mast.
>   I here am red, and there am green,
>   A beggar there and here a queen.
>   I sometimes live in house of hair,
>   And oft in hand of lady fair.
>   I please the young, I grace the old,
>   And am at once both hot and cold.
>   Say what I am then, if you can,
>   And find the rhyme, and you're the man."
>   (The Works of Jonathan Swift, D.D., Volume XV, p. 31)

The answer is "a fan", which a lady holds in her muff.

The great English actor, theatrical manager, and poet, David Garrick (1717-1779), was also known to engage in puzzling for entertainment. One enigma of his is particularly interesting, for it revolves around a situation rather than an object:

> "Kitty, a fair, but frozen maid,
>   Kindled a flame I still deplore;
>   The hood-wink'd boy I call'd in aid,
>   Much of his near approach afraid,
>   So fatal to my suit before.
>
> At length, propitious to my pray'r,
>   The little urchin came;
>   At once he sought the midway air,
>   And soon he clear'd, with dextrous care,
>   The bitter relicks of my flame.
>
> To Kitty, Fanny now succeeds,
>   She kindles slow, but lasting fires:
>   With care my appetite she feeds;
>   Each day some willing victim bleeds,
>   To satisfy my strange desires.
>
> Say, by what title, or what name,
>   Must I this youth address?

   Cupid and he are not the same,
   Tho' both can raise, or quench a flame --
    I'll kiss you, if you guess."
     (The Poetical Works of David Garrick, Esq., Volume II,
      London, George Kearsley, 1785, p. 507)

The enigmatic quality of Garrick's enigma is excellent, for many of
the lines of the verse have double meanings. The puzzle makes complete sense when the reader views it as being "written by a lady whose
maid had set her chimney on fire".

  Horatio Walpole (1717-1797), the English politician and man of
letters, is noted for the three enigmas which appear in his Works.
One was on "A Looking-Glass", and another on "A Sun-Dial". His
third enigma is this:

   " Before my birth I had a name,
   But soon as born I chang'd the same;
   And when I'm laid within the tomb,
   I shall my father's name assume.
   I change my name three days together,
   Yet live but one in any weather."
     (The Works of Horatio Walpole, Earl of Oxford, Volume
      IV, London, G.G. and J. Robinson, 1798, p. 404)

The enigma is answered by "to-day".

  The very popular English poet of the eighteenth century, William
Cowper (1731-1800), was also fond of word puzzles. In a letter written to the Rev. John Newton in July of 1780, Cowper included the following enigma, which is filled with paradoxical statements:

   "I am just two and two, I am warm, I am cold,
   And the parent of numbers that cannot be told.
   I am lawful, unlawful -- a duty, a fault,
   I am often sold dear, good for nothing when bought;
   An extraordinary boon, and a matter of course,
   And yielded with pleasure when taken by force."
     (John Bruce, The Poetical Works of William Cowper,
      Volume III, London, George Bell and Sons, 1896, p. 390)

The answer is "a kiss".

  Numerous other Britishers of note composed word puzzles during
the eighteenth century. Thus, puzzles were more than just a juvenile
amusement. Puzzling of the 1700s involved more than the riddles
and conundrums so popular with young people and common folk. If
puzzles were not universally looked upon as an art form, they were
at least viewed as an innocuous amusement that was of interest to the
intellectual as well as the average man. The 1797 edition of the Encyclopedia Britannica wrote of charades, which had become popular
only a number of years before, " The exercise of charades, if not

greatly constructive, is at least innocent and amusing. At all events,
as it has made its way into every fashionable circle, ... it will be
scarcely deemed unworthy of attention".

Evidently, however, the puzzles printed in the 1700s were not always of the highest literary quality, and already they were under attack
for being childish. The above article went on to say about the charade,
" The silliness indeed of most that have appeared in the papers under
this title, are not only destitute of all pleasantry in the stating, but
are formed in general of words utterly unfit for the purpose. They
have therefore been treated with the contempt they deserved" (" Charade", Encyclopedia Britannica III, 1797, p. 340).

Nineteenth-Century Puzzles   (William F. Shortz)

By the late 1700s and early 1800s, many new types of word puzzles had become popular in England. Charades began to rival enigmas and riddles in prevalence, and anagrams, transpositions, reversals, beheadments, and logogriphs all began to appear with greater and greater frequency.

Two puzzle books achieved a very wide sale in England during this period. The first one was The Masquerade, A Collection of New Enigmas, Logogriphs, Charades, Rebusses, Queries, and Transpositions, which was first published in 1797. New volumes of puzzles in the series were put out by the same editors in 1798, 1799, 1800, and 1801. The second book was A New Collection of Enigmas, Charades, Transpositions, &c., published in 1806. Both books undoubtedly introduced types of puzzles with which many Britishers had not yet become familiar.

The Masquerade went through an impressive series of editions, so it was clearly a popular publication. In the advertisement to the third edition of the second volume, the editors wrote, "A new edition is become necessary, on account of the increasing demand for this esteemed publication: and the Editors are happy that they are thus enabled to add to various other testimonies that of an extensive sale" (The Masquerade, Volume II, Southampton, George Wilkie, 1798, p. 3). And in the advertisement to the third volume, the editors wrote, "In publications of almost every kind, an extensive sale is allowed to be the best criterion of merit. This being premised, the Editors of the Masquerade have only to observe, that the friendly reception of their first volume ... -- and their second volume (tho' increased in number one half) having experienced very liberal patronage; -- they bring forward this their third volume with a considerable degree of confidence, having now printed more than double the number of the preceding year" (The Masquerade, Volume III, 1799, p. 3). The editors also claimed that all of their puzzles were original.

Two enigmas from the first volume of The Masquerade follow. The first one is fairly tricky, but not very difficult once the reader gets the idea. The second enigma contains some interesting contradictions which the reader is asked to resolve:

       "In camps about the centre I appear;
        In smiling meadows seen throughout the year;
        The silent angler views me in the streams,

And love-sick maidens in their morning dreams;
First in each mob conspicuous I stand,
Proud of the lead, and double in command;
Without my power no mercy can be shown,
Or soft compassion to their hearts be known;
Each sees me in himself, yet all agree
Their hearts and persons have no charms for me;
The chymist proves my virtue upon ore,
For touch'd by me, he changes it to more."
     (The Masquerade, Volume I, 1797, pp. 13-14)

" Tho' mean and humble is my birth,
   I sit enthroned on high --
My footsteps far above the earth,
   My canopy the sky:

O'er laboring subjects thus in state
   I bear despotic sway,
Yet on them condescend to wait,
   At break and close of day."
     (The Masquerade, Volume I, 1797, p. 21)

The answer to the first enigma is "the letter M", and the answer to the second is "a coachman".

Besides enigmas, The Masquerade also featured a large number of charades. That many of the charades were good ones attests to the fact that puzzles in popular publications were assuming a higher and higher quality. A simple, but interesting, charade in the first volume of The Masquerade follows:

" My first all sellers like to get,
   When they a bargain make;
My next they'll tell you in a pet
   That they will never take:

My whole is sure of names the worst
   By which we man can call
And he that is so far accurst
   Must be despised by all."
     (The Masquerade, Volume I, 1797, p. 50)

The charade is answered by the word "worthless".

Two other puzzles gaining acceptance during the late 1700s and early 1800s were transpositions (rearranging the letters of one word to form another) and reversals (reversing the letters of one word to form another). An example of each follows, the first from The Masquerade, and the second from A New Collection of Enigmas, Charades, Transpositions, &c.:

" Ye riddling fair, disclose my name,
   No doubt you quickly will descry it:

The self same characters proclaim
   The fruit, and how you'd wish to buy it."
      (The Masquerade, Volume III, 1799, p. 62)

" What skins of oranges are call'd
   If you (reverse), will show
The pow'r that seems most like to death
   Of any that we know."
      (A New Collection of Enigmas, Charades, Transposi-
      tions, &c., London, Longman, Hurst, Rees and Orme,
      1806, p. 191)

The answers are "peach-cheap" and "peels-sleep".

Next is a successive beheadment from the same period:

" Tho' small I am, yet, when entire,
I've force to set the world on fire.
Take off a letter, and 'tis clear
My paunch will hold a herd of deer:
Dismiss another, and you'll find
I once contain'd all human kind."
      (A New Collection of Enigmas, 1806, p. 190)

The beheadment is answered by "spark-park-ark".

The only other versified puzzle that was in vogue during the early
1800s was the logogriph. In this puzzle, the keyword was enigmatically
expressed, and then clues were given to other words which were composed of letters contained in the keyword. Thus, one logogriph appeared
in The Masquerade on the word "spear", which contains the letters
which form ape, spar, reap, asp, ear, rap, par, pear, pare, are, as,
sap, rasp, sea, pea, spa and spare. Logogriphs tended to be inordi-
nately long, as clues had to be given to each word contained in the
keyword. The logogriph was the forerunner of the numerical enigma,
which gained popularity in the mid-to-late 1800s, and the numerical
enigma was the forerunner of today's double acrostic.

Riddles and conundrums were just as popular as ever during the
early 1800s. An example from The Masquerade: " Why is a man
who has seen a young goat asleep, likely to give an account of a
stolen child?" " Because he has seen the kid-napping" (The Masquerade, Volume II, 1798, pp. 65, 81).

And an easy riddle:

" Pray tell me ladies, if you can,
Who is that highly favor'd man,
Who, tho' he's married many a wife,
May still live single all his life?"
      (The Masquerade, Volume III, 1799, p. 75)

Answer: "A clergyman".

And finally, anagrams to be solved were gaining great popularity. The best ones, of course, were those in which the anagrams were directly related to the transposed words. Thus, "To love ruin" could be rearranged to make REVOLUTION; "Great help" could be transposed to form TELEGRAPH; "Best in prayer" made PRESBY-TERIAN; "Hard case" made CHARADES; and "There we sat" could be anagrammed into SWEETHEART. All of these anagrams are fa-mous ones today, and all appeared in The Masquerade (The Mas-querade, Volume I, 1797, p. 73 and Volume II, 1798, p. 66).

These basic types of word puzzles, with the addition of a few other types, remained popular in Britain through the first half of the nineteenth century. A number of popular British magazines, such as The Penny Satirist, printed regular puzzle columns, and achieved good reader response. Puzzle books of excellent quality continued to appear, such as Riddles, Charades and Conundrums (1822), by John Winter Jones, and A Choice Collection of Riddles, Charades, and Conundrums (1834).

Just as many British writers and people of renown composed puz-zles during the eighteenth century, so it was during the first half of the nineteenth century. A number of noted men and women con-structed and solved puzzles for their amusement. Mrs. Anna Bar-bauld (1743-1825), a well-known English poet and miscellaneous writer, was a prolific composer of enigmas. One of her better works was this:

> " From rosy bowers we issue forth,
>   From east to west, from south to north;
> Unseen, unfelt, by night, by day,
> Abroad we take our airy way;
> We foster love and kindle strife,
> The bitter and the sweet of life;
> Piercing and sharp, we wound like steel --
> Now, smooth as oil, those wounds we heal;
> Not strings of pearl are valued more,
> Or gems encased in golden ore;
> Yet thousands of us every day,
> Worthless and vile, are thrown away.
> Ye wise, secure with bars of brass
> The double doors through which we pass;
> For, once escaped, back to our cell
> No human art can us compel."
>   ("Poetry, Anecdotes, &c.", Old Farmers' Alma-
>   nac, 1839, pages not numbered)

The enigma is answered by "words".

George Canning (1770-1827), the British statesman who served for a short period as Prime Minister of England, was also interested in word puzzles. His puzzle, which appears below, is one of the most famous of all word puzzles ever made:

" A word there is of plural number,
   Foe to ease and tranquil slumber;
   Any other word you take
   And add an s will plural make.
   But if you add an s to this,
   So strange the metamorphosis;
   Plural is plural now no more,
   And sweet what bitter was before."
         (William S. Walsh, Handy-Book of Literary Curiosi-
            ties, 1892, p. 301)

The answer is " cares - caress".

Winthrop Mackworth Praed (1802-1839) , an English author and politician, chiefly remembered for his humorous verse, was one of the greatest of all writers of enigmas and charades. The poetic style of his puzzles was of the highest quality found anywhere. Three of his puzzles are presented below. The first is a charade, which William Walsh calls " Praed's best, a really fine poem in itself":

" Come from my First, ay, come;
   The battle dawn is nigh
And the screaming trump and the thundering drum
   Are calling thee to die.
   Fight, as thy father fought;
   Fall, as thy father fell:
Thy task is taught, thy shroud is wrought;
   So forward and farewell!

   Toll ye my Second, toll;
   Fling high the flambeau's light;
And sing the hymn for a parted soul
   Beneath the silent night;
   The helm upon his head,
   The cross upon his breast,
Let the prayer be said, and the tear be shed:
   Now take him to his rest!

   Call ye my Whole, go call
   The lord of lute and lay,
And let him greet the sable pall
   With a noble song to-day;
   Ay, call him by his name,
   No fitter hand may crave
To light the flame of a soldier's fame
   On the turf of a soldier's grave!"
         (William S. Walsh, Handy-Book of Literary Curiosi-
            ties, 1892, pp. 147-148)

The charade is answered by "Campbell".

The second is one of the most controversial charades of all time, for many answers have been suggested for it, none of which is perfect. The charade is this:

"Sir Hilary charged at Agincourt;
    Sooth, 'twas an awful day!
And though in that old age of sport
The rufflers of the camp and court
    Had little time to pray.
'Tis said Sir Hilary muttered there
Two syllables by way of prayer:
    My First to all the brave and proud
    Who see to-morrow's sun:
My Next, with her cold and quiet cloud,
To those who find their dewy shroud
    Before to-day's be done:
And both together to all blue eyes
That weep when a warrior nobly dies."
          (The Poems of Winthrop Mackworth Praed, Volume II,
          London, Ward, Lock and Co., 187?, p. 387)

The answer generally accepted by most authorities is "Good-night".

The final puzzle is one of Praed's best enigmas. It is a story, containing an extended metaphor, written with excellent poetic style:

"A Templar kneeled at a Friar's knee;
He was a comely youth to see,
With curling locks, and forehead high,
And flushing cheek, and flashing eye;
And the Monk was as jolly and large a man
As ever laid lip to a convent can
    Or called for a contribution,
As ever read at midnight hour
    Confessional in lady's bower,
Ordained for a peasant the penance whip,
Or spoke for a noble's venial slip
    A venial absolution.

'O Father! in the dim twilight
I have sinned a grievous sin to-night;
And I feel hot pain e'er now begun
For the fearful murder I have done.

'I rent my victim's coat of green,
I pierced his neck with my dagger keen;
    The red stream mantled high:
I grasped him, Father, all the while,
With shaking hand, and feverish smile,
And said my jest, and sang my song,

And laughed my laughter, loud and long,
  Until his glass was dry!

'Though he was rich, and very old,
I did not touch a grain of gold,
But the blood I drank from the bubbling vein
Hath left on my lip a purple stain!'

'My son! my son! for this thou hast done,
Though the sands of thy life for aye should run,'
  The merry Monk did say,
'Though thine eye be bright, and thine heart be light,
Hot spirits shall haunt thee all the night,
  Blue devils all the day!'

The thunders of the Church were ended;
Back on his way the Templar wended;
But the name of him the Templar slew
Was more than the Inquisition knew."
    (The Poems of Winthrop Mackworth Praed, Volume II,
    187?, p. 388-389)

What the Templar actually "slew" was "a bottle".

Among the many other noted men and women in England during the
early 1800s who wrote enigmas and charades, we might mention the
following: Lord Macaulay, the English historian, essayist and politician; Miss Hannah Moore, popular poetess; Charles S. Calverley,
well-known poet; and the Rev. Richard Barham, author of the Ingold-
sby Legends. The list is impressive, and indicates the extent to
which word puzzles had gained popularity in Britain in the early
nineteenth century.

What place did word puzzles hold in British society during this
period? John Winter Jones, in the introduction to his book Riddles,
Charades, and Conundrums, gives us a glimpse of the answer to that
question. Even though many learned Englishmen, as we have already
seen, enjoyed word puzzles and constructed them for their own amusement, word puzzles were generally under attack for being a childish
diversion. John Winter Jones seemed to take the defensive in uphold-
ing the value of puzzles when he wrote, "...this species of writing ...
not withstanding the laugh that may be raised against it, is still cher-
ished by the lively and the young. None can dispute that riddles are
at least an innocent amusement; and when tolerably well chosen, they
prove an exercise of ingenuity, and must have a tendency to teach the
mind to compare and judge. It has, perhaps, been owing to the trash
commonly disseminated under the name of enigmas, that they have
fallen into disrepute" (John Winter Jones, Riddles, Charades, and
Conundrums, the Greater Part of Which Have Never Been Published,
London, F. Marshall, 1822, pp. v-vi). Thus, puzzles in many popular publications were of poor quality and were, perhaps, rightly considered childish amusements. The best puzzles, however, were far
from childish; they were an art through which many of the leading
intellectuals of the times entertained themselves.

PANGRAMS

Pangrams -- sentences in which each letter of the alphabet is used exactly once -- have been around for many years. Although a definitive article on their history has never, to my knowledge, been written, attempts to create pangrams go back at least a century. In A Budget of Paradoxes (Dover reprint, 1954), the famous English mathematician Augustus De Morgan mentions that he and William Whewell once amused themselves by trying to construct a pangram. I, QUARTZ PYX, WHO FLING MUCK BEDS, the best they could come up with, is a 26-letter sentence in which an extra I and U are substituted for J and V (in ancient inscriptions, these letters were interchangeable). Unfortunately, pangrams often require a good bit of explanation before their meaning is clear to the uninitiated. De Morgan's comments are typical:

> I long thought that no human being could say this under any circumstances. At last I happened to be reading a religious writer -- as he thought himself -- who threw aspersions on his opponents thick and threefold. Heyday! came into my head, this fellow flings muck beds; he must be a quartz pyx. And then I remembered that a pyx is a sacred vessel, and quartz is a hard stone, as hard as the heart of a religious foe-curser. So that the line is the motto of the ferocious sectarian, who turns his religious vessels into mud-holders, for the benefit of those who will not see what he sees.

One way out of this obscurity is to allow some letters to be used more than once. It is surprising how few additional letters are needed; here is a sampling of the best ones of various lengths:

WALTZ, NYMPH, FOR QUICK JIGS VEX BUD (28)
HOW QUICKLY DAFT JUMPING ZEBRAS VEX (30)
JACKDAWS LOVE MY BIG SPHINX OF QUARTZ (31)
PACK MY BOX WITH FIVE DOZEN LIQUOR JUGS (32)

The jackdaws pangram is cited in the Guinness Book of World Records without attribution; Marvin Moore of Estacada, Oregon claims to have originated it (Oregon Journal, July 8, 1968).

Pangram Variations

Pangrammatic research has been hampered by the requirement that reasonable sentences be formed. One can define a whole constellation of interesting investigations if one concentrates on the words making up a pangram without insisting that they have a collective meaning.

First it is necessary to define the stockpile of words out of which pangrams can be formed. To fix ideas, we allow only those words appearing in boldface type in the Merriam-Webster Pocket Dictionary, or readily inferred forms (noun plurals and verb endings in -S, -ED or -ING). Other than I and A, we do not allow single letters of the alphabet to be regarded as words; similarly, we disallow prefixes, suffixes, and words that appear only as part of multi-word phrases.

What is the smallest number of words into which the letters of the alphabet can be anagrammed? The answer is a bit unexpected: there is no collection of Pocket Webster words that can be formed in this manner. The nearest approach is 25 letters, as illustrated by CHINTZ PLUMBS FJORD GAWKY VEX. Nevertheless, the failure to achieve perfection suggests a new avenue of inquiry; what is the largest number of different letters of the alphabet, each used once, that can be anagrammed into four words? three words? two words? one word? The final question can be rephrased in a more familiar form: what is the longest isogram in Webster's Pocket Dictionary? In short, isograms and pangrams are the limiting cases of a series of challenging word-problems which have not been previously explored.

The longest isogram in the Pocket Dictionary is well-known: the 14-letter AMBIDEXTROUSLY. It is unlikely that two words can utilize more than 19 letters, as illustrated by BLACKSMITH GUNPOW-DER. The three-word record is presently 22, as exemplified by HUMPBACKS FROWZY TINGLED, and the four-word record of 24 is given by HUMPBACKS FROWZY VELDT JINX. Other combinations of words can be found which achieve these letter-scores.

Let us now eliminate the requirement that each letter of the alphabet can be used only once, and ask how many different letters of the alphabet can be used in one, two, three, ... words. We expect to do somewhat better than the 14, 19, 22, ... different letters established above. However, we are surprised once more; the improvement is modest or non-existent. To begin with, there does not appear to be any word in the Pocket Dictionary which uses 15 (or more) different letters; no doubt this is a consequence of the relatively small number of words of 16 or more letters. For two words, a one-letter improvement is possible: AMBIDEXTROUSLY WATCHMAKING uses 20 different letters. For three words, the best set may be the 23-letter AMBIDEXTROUSLY FOREKNOWLEDGE RECEIVERSHIP, again a one-letter improvement.

If four or more words are allowed, it is possible to use all 26 letters of the alphabet, and the criterion of excellence must be changed from the number of different letters used to the minimum number of total letters used. The four-word record of 39 letters seems amenable to improvement: ZIPPING FOXHOUND JABBERWOCKY VENTRILO-QUISM. The five-word record of 29 letters is somewhat more secure: PLUMBING CHINTZY SQUAWK FJORD VEX. If six words are allowed, the absolute minimum of 27 letters is reached: LAMB SQUAWK FJORD CHINTZ VEX GYP.

What are the analogous results if a larger dictionary is used? We enlarge the stockpile of words to include the Second and Third Editions of Webster's Unabridged, while retaining the various restrictions introduced earlier. Unfortunately, there is no easy way to locate groups of words having the required properties; therefore, many of the results below must be regarded as preliminary, subject to improvement by the diligent dictionary-searcher.

To begin with, it is now possible to find a set of words which exhausts the alphabet; Dmitri Borgmann has come up with the five-word PHLEGMS FYRD WUZ QVINT JACKBOX.

The longest isogram in Webster's is generally recognized to be the 15-letter DERMATOGLYPHICS, an improvement of only one letter over the Pocket Dictionary entry. The two words BLACKSMITH GUNPOWDERY utilize 20 letters, again only a one-letter gain. One can speculate on the possibility of finding three words which use 23 letters, or four words which use 25, but it has proved impossible to find any examples.

If letters can be used more than once, there are a handful of Websterian words which use 16 different letters, the shortest of which appears to be SUPERACKNOWLEDGMENT. Ralph Beaman proposes FORMALDEHYDESULPHOXYLIC VENTRILOQUIZING as a two-word combination having 22 different letters which should be difficult to beat; however, a pair of words using fewer total letters might be found.

When three or four words are allowed, all 26 letters can be included. This problem was first investigated in the May and August 1972 Word Ways; Mary Hazard proposed the four-word 31-letter set JACKBOX VIEWFINDERS PHLEGMY QUARTZ, and Darryl Francis discovered JUXTAPYLORIC QUICK-FLOWING SEMIBOLSHEVIZED, a three-word set with 39 letters. Subsequently, he lowered the letter-count to 36 with BENZOXYCAMPHORS QUICK-FLOWING JUVENTUDE.

If open sources are allowed, it is possible to find a set of four words which uses the 26 letters of the alphabet. Dmitri Borgmann suggests FJORDHUNGKVISL (a short river in central Iceland, listed in Volume 3 of the Times Atlas of the World), PECQ (a town in western Belgium, near the French border, also listed in Volume 3 of the Times Atlas), WAMB (an obsolete spelling of womb, in Webster's Second) and ZYXT (an obsolete Kentish second person singular indicative present form of the verb see, the last word in the Oxford English Dictionary).

Dmitri Borgmann has also constructed a set of three words containing the alphabet which uses only 28 letters: FJORDHUNGKVISL, EXPECTABLY, and MQWZ, the last word being a reformed spelling of the word mows using a method developed by Fred S. C. Wingfield a generation ago (see page 288 of H. L. Mencken's The American Language, Supplement II).

□ "JUMP, dogs! Why vex Fritz Blank, QC?" Does anyone claim copyright on this? Or can I have half the royalties to Lolita? — *(Rev) Sydney Knight, Elvington, York.*

A pangrammatic crossword (Word Ways, February 1970) can be viewed as a word list containing all the letters of the alphabet, together with a few repeated letters. However, few word lists of this nature can be converted into a pangrammatic crossword; no letter can appear more than twice in the list, and those that do appear twice must be suitably placed so that the words can be interlocked. If the crossword consists of branches without any closed loops (the usual pangrammatic state of affairs), the number of extra letters must be one less than the number of words. From this fact, one can immediately deduce that the least number of words that can appear in a pangrammatic crossword is five; a four-word pangrammatic crossword would require a total of only 29 letters, two less than the record established by Mary Hazard. Leslie Card of Urbana, Illinois has constructed two five-word pangrammatic crosswords based on Webster's Second or Third Edition:

```
C                       S
H                       J
L                       W A Q F
W A Q F     J           M
M           V O X       L   B       V
Y           K           U N C O P Y R I G H T E D
S P I T Z E N B U R G   X   K       Z
            D
```

Still other pangram variations are possible. In the February 1968 Word Ways, it was pointed out that players of the game of Jotto find it useful to construct sets of five-letter isograms with no letters in common. Howard Bergerson came up with a set of five such words from Webster's Second (see below). The Jotto problem can be generalized to words of other lengths: 4 six-letter words and 6 four-letter words, 3 seven-letter words and 7 (or δ) three-letter words:

NTH VEX JUG RIP ADZ SKY FOB (CWM)
CYST FLEX WHIZ JUMP KNOB DRAG
FUDGY JAMBS PHLOX WRECK QVINT
MUZJIK PEGBOX-DWARFS LYNCHT
JACKBOX FRESHLY DUMPING

3330 Pangrams

How many different pangrams are possible? Very few are found in the literature of recreational linguistics; therefore, it may be somewhat surprising to the average person that thousands of pangrams can be constructed. Using a computer tape of words in Webster's Second Edition prepared by the Air Force in the 1960s, Dennis Ritchie of Bell Telephone Laboratories programmed a computer to search for pangrams and came up with 3330 of them. Many more are possible, for the Air Force tape omits most Websterian words (below the line) that are variant spellings, Biblical names, or reformed spellings -- including such prime pangrammatic possibilities as QVINT (var. of kvint), SUQ (var. of sooq), WUZ (dial. var. of was), and WAQF (var. of wakf).

Specifically, Ritchie gave the computer two tasks: (1) generate a list of pangrams consisting of words of two or more letters using all 26 letters; (2) generate a list of pangrams consisting of the isolated letter S plus words of two or more letters using the remaining 25 letters. The latter list can be converted to a legitimate pangram list by using the letter S as a plural or a verb ending on one of the other words. He found 2005 pangrams of the former type and 1325 of the latter; no attempt has been made to determine the actual number of different pangrams possible by alternative assignments of the letter S.

This article describes various characteristics of this pangram list, recognizing that the results are critically dependent upon the stock of words used to form pangrams. For example, consider the number of words needed to form a pangram: there are 104 pangrams of six words and 3226 pangrams of seven words, but if the single word CWM is banned from the stockpile, there are only 250 pangrams left, of which 92 contain six words and 158, seven words. On the other hand, if the word SUQ is added, it is easy to find the eight word pangram CWM NTH VERD SUQ JIB FOLK GYP ZAX, and Dmitri Borgmann has used WUZ and QVINT to find the five-word pangram QVINT WUZ JACKBOX PHLEGM FYRDS.

CWM is by far the most prevalent word in the list of pangrams, occurring in 92 per cent of them; other common words are QOPH (65 per cent) and JYNX (52 per cent). In fact, 44 per cent of the pangrams contain all three of these words! Four other words -- QUNG, SHOQ, VEXT and VEX -- appear in at least 10 per cent of the pangrams. On the other hand, some words appear in only one pangram in the entire list.

Because Q ordinarily requires two vowels to follow it, there are very few Q-words suitable for pangrams. 3307 of the 3330 pangrams use either QOPH, SHOQ, QUNG or QURSH; the remaining 23 are scattered among SQUDGY (12 examples), QUIZ (4 examples), SQUDGE, SQUAB, QUAB, QUAK, QUARK, SQUARK and QUINK.

Unless the pangram has only six words, including a Q-word which uses only one vowel, it is clear that one or more words of the pangram must be vowelless (no AEIOUY). The great scarcity of vowelless words in Webster's accounts for the heavy use of CWM alluded to earlier. CRWTH appears in 166 pangrams, and NTH in 11 (always in conjunction with CWM). There are 84 pangrams in which all the words have at least one vowel.

Despite the great overlap in words, it is possible to locate five pangrams with no words in common:

shoq fjeld vug zink pyx brat cwm

Qung fjord vext biz swack lymph
qursh Jynx veldt zimb gowf pack
qoph jambs vex Fritz wynd gluck
squdgy job vamp knez flix crwth

Surprisingly, the Borgmann pangram cited earlier has no word in common with any of these.

The longest word appearing in any pangram of the list is SCHMALTZ
and the second-longest is BASHLYK:

job Qung verd schmaltz pyx fowk
fjord Qung vext zip bashlyk cwms

No pangram is entirely in Webster's Pocket Dictionary; the closest
one is FJORD QUIZ VEX BALKS NTH GYP CWM, lacking only the last
word. (Note that the letter S can be appended to several other words,
leading to minor variations.) A small number of pangrams, however,
are entirely in Webster's Collegiate:

jab qoph vug Fritz lynx desk cwm
jug qoph vex blitz fry dank cwms
jug qoph vex blintz fard sky cwm
jug qoph vex Fritz bland sky cwm
fjord quiz vex balk gyp nth cwms

fjeld qursh vat zig pyx knob cwm
junk qoph vex Fritz by glad cwms
junk qoph vex blitz dry fag cwms
junk qoph vex blitz fry gad cwms
jag qoph vex blitz fry dunk cwms

jag qoph vex blitz dry funk cwms
jag qoph vex blintz fry dusk cwm
jib qoph vug zed kraft lynx cwms
Jud qoph vex blintz fry skag cwm

The last pangram contains JUD, a short form of Judson which (like
Fritz) appears in the given names appendix of the Collegiate; the
word SKAG is not in the Seventh Edition of the Collegiate, but can
be found in the Pocket Dictionary.

Literary Pangrams

If one examines a sufficiently long section of English-language text, it is virtually certain that all letters of the alphabet will occur in it.   For example, it has been claimed that every letter of the alphabet appears on every page of Webster's Collegiate Dictionary.   To put this claim in perspective, Leslie E. Card of Urbana, Illinois examined 58 pages of the Pocket Webster Dictionary, and discovered that eight of these were not pangrammatic (Z is missing on pages 107, 193 and 541; Q is missing on pages 11 and 173; X is missing on pages 3 and 113; and both Q and X are missing on page 29).

How many consecutive letters of text must be examined before there is a 50 per cent chance of sampling the entire alphabet? This question can be answered theoretically, by making certain assumptions about letter-frequencies and independence, or practically, by counting letters in literary passages until all letters appear.

The four rarest letters in English-language text are Z (which appears with probability .0006, or approximately once every 1700 letters), Q (probability .0010), J (probability .0010) and X (probability .0016); all other letters are so likely to appear by the time that Z, Q, J and X have all been found that they can be neglected in the calculation.   If one is willing to pretend that English-language text can be modeled by a random process in which letters are independently selected according to the above probabilities, the probability that no Z, Q, X or J appear in a string of n letters is given by the formula

$$P = 1 - (1 - (1 - .0006)^n)(1 - (1 - .001)^n)(1 - (1 - .001)^n) \cdot (1 - (1 - .0016)^n)$$

If different trial values of n are inserted in this equation and the corresponding values of P calculated, one discovers that a sample of about 2000 letters is needed to have a 50 per cent chance of including the entire alphabet.

But is the random model a reasonable one? Probably not, because different authors have different vocabularies; furthermore, the text may deal with such topics as queens, organizations or jokes, raising the probability of encountering rare letters.   Even if these difficulties are ignored, the independence assumption is a questionable one.   Z, the rarest letter, frequently appears doubled in a word, suggesting that the distance between successive Z-words is more than 1700 letters.

Ralph Beaman of Boothwyn, Pennsylvania took a sample of 25 pangrammatic passages from several newspapers and magazines, discovering that their lengths ranged from 750 to 8000-plus letters with a median of 2500 letters.   This seems like a more reasonable value than 2000.

A more interesting question, however, is: how short a string of letters can one find in a literary work which uses all the letters? In Language on Vacation (Scribner's, 1965), Dmitri Borgmann cited a 76-letter pangrammatic sentence from Sarah Grand's The Beth Book, published in New York in 1897:

> It was an exquisitely deep blue just then, with filmy white clouds
> drawn up over it like gauze

Actually, the alphabet is contained in a letter-sequence only 67 letters
long, from the X in exquisitely to the Z in gauze.

The odds against the inadvertent creation of a 67-letter literary
pangram are undoubtedly astronomical; one suspects that Sarah Grand
may have deliberately constructed this curiosity. Andrew Griscom of
Menlo Park, California succeeded in finding a 139-letter pangrammatic
letter-sequence in Jane Austen's Mansfield Park (page 321 of the Pen-
guin edition):

> ... just to be denied. But there is no time fixed, perhaps tomor-
> row, or whenever your spirits are composed enough. For the
> present you have only to tranquillize yourself. Check ...

One must admire the patient devotion of a logophile who can read the
immortal Jane Austen with one lobe of his brain while scanning her
paragraphs for pangrams with the other!

PENCIL-AND-PAPER WORD GAMES

The purpose of this article is to describe the rules and strategy for a number of pencil-and-paper word games scattered through the literature. Before embarking upon this task, however, it is necessary to define terms and give general background appropriate to word games.

Broadly speaking, word games can be divided into two types: those that require (at most) pencil and paper to play, and those that require additional equipment, such as cards, dice, lettered tiles, timers, playing boards and the like. The latter games are ordinarily manufactured and sold by commercial firms, and the former are not, but there are exceptions on both sides. On the one hand, Probe and My Word! are elaborate versions of Hangman and Crash, respectively, and could be played by someone possessing the rules but nothing more of the commercial game. On the other hand, various non-commercial games requiring a set of lettered tiles to play have been devised; I note Word Poker and Scrabble variations in the May 1971 and August 1974 Word Ways, and Anagrab, Pontlevis and Take and Make in the December 1974, May 1976 and January 1976 issues of Games & Puzzles. (Quirk, in the July 1974 Games & Puzzles, requires even more: eight lettered dice plus a special playing board with transparent overlay.) These games are not discussed further here.

Pencil-and-paper word games can be played in a wide variety of environments awkward for board games: on the beach, in an automobile or train, etc. Some can even be played while taking a walk! A more basic distinction between the two types of games is the role of chance: in pencil-and-paper games, one is solely matching one's skill and knowledge against that of an opponent, but in games using tiles, cards or dice this skill is somewhat diluted by the luck of the draw. (In the best word games of this type, such as Scrabble, the leveling process of chance does not go very far; the more skilled player is overwhelmingly likely to be the winner.)

A game requires a sequence of responses of each opponent to the actions of the other. The two players (or more) need not be in the same room, however; games can be played more slowly by mail. As long as this interaction occurs, one or more of the players can be represented by a digital computer suitably programmed to respond to moves. However, a contest in which a person matches wits against Nature (for example, forms as many words as possible out of the letters in confidential) or an impersonal formulator who requires no further consultation (for example, solves crossword puzzles or cryptograms) is not considered to be a game.

In many pencil-and-paper games, the roles of the two players are symmetric; moves of similar type are alternately made, and the only distinction is who gets to move first. In other pencil-and-paper games, however, the roles of the adversaries are asymmetric: one person selects a word, and the other attempts to guess it under certain restrictions, the first player telling him of his success or failure as he progresses. Symmetry is restored to games of this type by playing the game in pairs, with each person alternately word-selector and word-guesser.

It is difficult to identify the original inventors of some pencil-and-paper word games; very likely several have been independently proposed in slightly different forms by many people over the years. Nevertheless, it is worth giving recognition to Dave Silverman of West Los Angeles, California, a fecund inventor who has described several of the games given below in the Kickshaws column of Word Ways. (He is also the author of a book on games in general, Your Move, published by McGraw-Hill in 1972.) Other games have appeared in the magazine Games & Puzzles, or have been developed by members of NOST (Knights Of the Square Table), a group of people who play an incredible variety of games with each other by mail. (Since March 1976 a separate column in their monthly newsletter NOST-Algia has been devoted to word games.)

In the 1940s, John von Neumann and Oskar Morgenstern authored the Theory of Games and Economic Behavior, a landmark book which develops in mathematical language the idea of a game as a two-player zero-sum (your gain is my loss) contest, in which each player selects a strategy (a complete list of moves, including responses to all possible opponent moves) at random from a predetermined list of such strategies. The central theorem of the von Neumann-Morgenstern theory says (1) Player 1 can randomly select strategies from his list in such a manner that his gain is, on the average, at least a certain value, regardless of the strategies chosen by Player 2; (2) Player 2 can similarly select strategies so that, on the average, his loss is less than or equal to a certain value, regardless of what Player 1 does; (3) the minimum possible gain guaranteed to Player 1 equals the maximum possible loss guaranteed to Player 2 (this is called the "value of the game"). However, if either player deviates from optimum play in selecting his strategies, his opponent can take advantage of this to raise his gain or lower his loss.

While their formulation of a game had enormous theoretical impact upon the further mathematical development of game theory, it has proven impossible to list the strategies and the random method for choosing them except for a few very simple games. This is especially true for word games as opposed to mathematical ones, for the former are typically much less patterned than the latter: in word games, moves are constrained by the necessity to form words, which are very irregularly distributed in word space (as a simple example of word space, think of two-letter words plotted as points on a two-dimensional grid in which the first letter is plotted on the horizontal axis and the second letter on the vertical axis). The experienced word gamester is able to exploit this irregularity to his advantage, but it is usually impossible to write down an optimum strategy for doing so in succinct form.

It should be emphasized that the inability to specify the optimum strategy is what makes a game interesting to play -- if the strategy were known to both players, there would be no need to play the game at all, as the result (the value of the game) is predetermined. Tic-tac-toe, for example, is uninteresting to play once both players discover that optimum play guarantees a draw. The advent of the computer, which can evaluate optimum strategies previously beyond human ken, threatens to make additional games trivial and uninteresting.

Sometimes, however, the strategies appropriate to a word game can be exhibited by drastically simplifying the game. This can be done by limiting the vocabulary size allowed, and, in games in which only words of a certain length are used, by considering shorter words. From considering strategies in simpler games, one can sometimes formulate general principles useful in realistic ones.

For those who are serious players of word games, looking carefully for good strategies, it is usually more enjoyable to play with opponents of equal caliber. If there are more than two players in the game, one is sometimes frustrated by an inept player unwittingly giving an advantage to one of the other opponents. Also, it is most important that the allowable stockpile of words be carefully defined beforehand -- usually, words listed in boldface in a specified dictionary. If inferred words are to be allowed (plurals of nouns, -s, -ed, -ing endings on verbs, etc.) this should be explicitly stated.

HANGMAN

Description: In this non-symmetric n-person game, one player writes down a target word on a concealed slip of paper and announces the number of letters it contains. The other players take turns guessing if it contains a given letter: if it does, the first player fills in all occurrences of the letter in their proper positions, but if it does not, the guesser is scored a demerit. Players continue to guess letters in turn until the target word has been revealed; then a new player from the group thinks of a fresh target word. A player is eliminated from the game when he has accumulated a given number of demerits; the last survivor is the winner.

Variations: (1) Instead of filling in multiple occurrences of a repeated letter, the first player can fill in a single occurrence of his choice. (2) Instead of filling in all occurrences in their proper positions, the first player announces the number of occurrences of the letter in the word. In this variant, it is sufficient to identify the word or a transposal of it forming another word.

(3) The first player is allowed to alter his target word as the game progresses, so long as the alteration is consistent with all previously-guessed letters.

This well-known parlor game takes its name from the way in which demerits are usually scored -- by drawing parts of a man (head, eyes, nose, mouth, trunk, arms, legs, etc.) suspended from a gallows each time a demerit is scored. Although it might appear that the best strategy of the player proposing the word is to find a long one, success is often achieved with shorter words having many alternate possibilities in one or more positions (such as -IGHT) or words containing repetitions of a rare letter plus common letters in common positions (such as GIGGLED or FIFE).

GHOST

Description: In this symmetric n-person game, players take turns adding letters in a sequence from left to right (C, CI, CIS, ...). If the letter added by a player converts the sequence into a word of three or more letters, he earns a demerit. Each time a player adds a letter, he can be challenged by the next player in turn to produce a word beginning with that sequence; if he can do so, the challenger is given a demerit but if he cannot he is given a demerit. The person to complete a word or the challenger starts a new sequence. A player is eliminated from the game when he has accumulated a given number of demerits; the last survivor is the winner.

Variations: (1) Letters can be added either at the beginning or the end of the sequence (Superghost).
(2) The letters of the sequence can be transposed to form a word.

Superghost, known to word buffs for many years, was amusingly described by the late James Thurber in his short story " Do You Want to Make Something Out of It?", found in Thurber Country (1953):

" The Superghost aficionado is a moody fellow, given to spelling to himself at table, not listening to his wife, and staring dully at his frightened children, wondering why he didn't detect, in yesterday's game, that 'cklu' is the guts of 'lacklustre', and priding himself on having stumped everybody with 'nehe' the middle of 'swineherd'. In this last case, 'bonehead' would have done, since we allow slang if it is in the dictionary, but 'Stonehenge' is out, because we don't allow proper nouns. "

It is good strategy to bluff by adding a letter to the sequence instead of meekly completing a word; the next player may see a word in the sequence, or, even if he does not, may fear to risk losing a challenge and bluff a letter himself. When playing a game of Ghost as a boy with my father, I was confronted with the next move in the sequence BAU. Realizing that BAUBLE would end on me, and unable to think of another word, I desperately added an X, unwittingly converting it to BAUXITE, a word my father knew which changed a loss for me into a win. (Ordinarily, it is better strategy to bluff with a

more common letter.) In adding letters to the sequence, it is good
strategy to restrict the word alternatives, avoiding if possible any
that end on you.

With sufficient research, one can ascertain safe and unsafe opening letters for Ghost with respect to the dictionary being used; for
example, Darryl Francis determined that all letters but L are unsafe for the first player (using uncapitalized boldface words in Webster's Third Unabridged), as the second one can at once narrow the
possibilities to words of odd length. Similarly, it has been discovered
that all letters but H, J and M are unsafe for the first player in a two-
player game of Ghost, and all letters but A and O are unsafe for the
first player in a two-player game of Superghost, if unhyphenated boldface words in Webster's Pocket Dictionary (1970 edition) are used.
The detailed strategies, which occupy several pages, can be found in
the November 1971 and February 1973 Word Ways. Obviously, if
both players have access to such strategies, the game of Ghost becomes about as interesting and challenging as Tic-tac-toe.

THE LAST WORD

Description: In this symmetric two-person game, the first player
selects a word of n letters beginning with A. The second player selects a word of n letters that occurs later in the dictionary and has
one or more crashes (occurrences of the same letter in the same
position) with the preceding word. The players continue to play alternately in this manner until one finds it impossible to locate a word
with these characteristics; he is the loser.

Variations: (1) The loser is the last player to have a legal play
available to him.
(2) Each word must have one or more letters in common with the
preceding word, but these do not have to be in the same positions.
(3) Each word must have one or more letters in common with the
preceding word, but none of these can be in the same positions.

The basic game was first described by Dave Silverman in the
May 1970 Word Ways. In all these games, one can in principle
work out trees of possible moves, exhibiting safe and unsafe words
for the first player; it is then a trivial matter for the first player to
start with a safe word beginning with A, if one exists. For example,
in a regular game restricted to 24 common two-letter words

am	as	be	do	he	in	it	my	of	or	to	us
an	at	by	go	if	is	me	no	on	so	up	we

words terminating the game are it, my, or, to, us and we, and
nearly all the other words can be converted in one step to these; in
fact, the only two which cannot are an and am, safe starting words
for the first player. In the first variation, safe words are those
which can only be converted to the six terminating words: me, up,
is, on, so, at; therefore, the first player should always play at.
Am, an and as are unsafe, for the second player can respond with at,

forcing the first player to it .

Safe words are far more difficult to find if words of three or more letters are used, and the game is correspondingly more interesting to play. It is conjectured that safe words for the first player beginning with A always exist; the problem is to locate them, together with the correct responses to each move the second player can make.

TIC-TAC-TOE GAMES

Description: In this symmetric two-person game, the stockpile of allowed words is ARMY, CHAT, FISH, GIRL, HORN, KNIT, SOUP, SWAN and VOTE. Each player in turn draws a word from the stockpile, and the first person to collect three words sharing a common letter is the winner.

Description: In this symmetric two-person game, the stockpile of allowed words is APE, BUD, CAN, DAY, DIE, DOT, HOP, LIP, ONE, PUT, RAT, RIG, ROW, RUE, SUN and TIN. Each player in turn draws a word from the stockpile. First player (the Toiler) wins if either player gathers four words sharing a common letter; second player (the Spoiler) wins if neither player has four words sharing a common letter after all sixteen have been drawn.

Variation: Spoiler plays first instead of Toiler.

Both of these games are disguised versions of Tic-tac-toe, as can be demonstrated by properly arranging the word stockpiles in square arrays:

fish	soup	swan		ape	day	can	rat
girl	horn	army		lip	die	tin	rig
knit	vote	chat		hop	dot	one	row
				put	bud	sun	rue

The three-by-three game is described as Game 48 in Your Move, and the four-by-four game, also devised by Dave Silverman, appears in the May 1972 Word Ways. Like Tic-tac-toe, the three-by-three game will always end in a draw if both players play optimally; however, a knowledgeable player will beat one that is unaware of the game's structure five times out of six, going either first or second. The four-by-four game, in which a draw is not possible, can always be won by Toiler; contrariwise, Spoiler can always win the variation (proof of both assertions has been developed by Garry Crum of Louisville, Ohio). However, the strategies to be followed are in both cases so involved that this word game, unlike the first one, is likely to appeal to the casual player even after its pattern is revealed.

CRASH and JOTTO

Description: In this asymmetric two-person game, one player writes down an n-letter target word on a slip of paper; the other player attempts to guess it by suggesting n-letter test words. For each test word, the first player reports the number of crashes (occurrences of the same letter in the same position between the test and target words -- ONE and TEN have no crashes, FOUR and FIVE have one); the second player is scored by the number of test words he requires to obtain an n-crash (an identification of the target word). The players then reverse their roles, and the winner is the one with the lower score.

Variations: (1) The first player reports the number of letters in common between the test and target words, without regard to their positions (Jotto, Secret Word).
(2) The first player is allowed to change the target word during the course of the game, as long as it is consistent with the number of crashes reported for all earlier test words (Wild Crash).
(3) The first player reveals his word, and players alternately add n-letter words to the list which have no crashes with any earlier word on the list. The first player unable to add another word with this property loses (Uncrash).
(4) The first player thinks of a target sentence of four words and writes it down on a slip of paper; the second player attempts to guess the sentence with test sentences. For each test sentence, the first player tells the second whether each word is earlier or later in the dictionary than the corresponding word in the test sentence. The object is for the second player to discover the sentence with as few tests as possible (The Game of Convergence).

Crash, the basic game, is a sophisticated version of Hangman in which one is not allowed to guess individual letters of the target word, but must infer them from the often-ambiguous clues provided by the number of crashes with test words. To speed up the game, particularly if it is played by mail (as NOST does), test words can be salvoed and scored together -- 5 words the first time, 4 the second, etc. Games in which n is equal to five appear to be the most popular.

The strategy of Crash is quite complex. To illustrate the nuances which arise, we discuss strategies for a simple game, using as a dictionary the 24 common two-letter words listed in The Last Word earlier. In this game, the player choosing the target word must randomize his choice, and the player attempting to locate it by a series of test words must randomize his sequence; otherwise, each player can take advantage of the other's regularities to increase (or decrease) the average number of test words needed for target identification.

A Crash strategy for the two-letter word version can be succinctly represented by the sequence of test words offered if no crashes occur. When one crash does occur, the branching strategy path is easy to infer: determine which letter caused the crash by means of two appropriate test words, and then test all words containing the relevant letter. (For example, if in generates a crash, try it and an; if an also generates a crash, try all other words ending with n.)

In a good strategy, test words are selected to eliminate as many remaining alternatives as possible if no crash occurs -- thus, it is desirable to start with a word like is, which will eliminate five other words (as, us, if, in, it) if there is no crash, rather than up, which eliminates only us. Typical strategies of this sort are listed below, with the number of words eliminated by each crash failure in parentheses:

    an (6), so (5), be (5), if (4), us (2), or, my
    is (6), so (5), be (5), an (4), of (2), up, my
    in (6), so (5), be (5), as (4), of (2), up, my

Note that symmetries allow certain substitutions to be made in these strategies: do, to, go or no for so; me for be; or for of. These strategies require no more than seven test words to identify any target word; the average number of steps needed (if the target word is selected at random -- that is, each of the 24 words has an equal chance of being picked) is slightly less than 4.4, the minimum possible value. However, an alert opponent will quickly start selecting words like my, up, or and of since these are typically found late in the above strategies. What is needed is a group of strategies such that, if each strategy in the group is picked with a certain probability, the average number of test words required to identify a target word is constant, no matter what target word is selected. Unfortunately, the optimal strategies and their proper mix cannot be easily determined even for this simple game without the aid of a computer. However, the following pair of strategies (each one used at random half the time) offers some improvement:

    us (4), of (4), so (5), be (5), my, an (4), it
    an (6), no (5), is (4), we (5), by, or (2), up

Although the average number of steps needed to find a randomly-chosen target has risen from 4.4 to 4.65, no target requires (on the average) more than 5.5 steps. If the player who selects the target word knows that his opponent is using the above pair of strategies, the best he can do is select do, so, go, to, no, be, me, we, he, it and in at random; the two strategies require an average of 5.5 steps to locate each of these eleven words. To gain this additional advantage of .85 steps, however, the target setter takes a big risk; he cannot afford to play these eleven words exclusively, lest his opponent discover this and switch to the new strategy

    so (5), be (4), it (2)

which, on the average, requires less than 3.3 steps to detect the target.

In the postal version of Crash, one has plenty of time to work out strategy between moves. Garry Crum suggests that the first salvo of five test words should be selected to minimize the maximum number of words left to be guessed, regardless of the crash pattern. Unfortunately, it is a tedious task to check out possible five-word salvos. He claims that AERIE FIERY CRIER BOAST SAUTE leaves a maximum of 85 words to be further checked (using the Pocket Webster Dictionary) no matter what pattern of crashes and non-crashes is

reported. However, one needs several more lists of this quality to
select from at random so that the opponent cannot tailor his target
word to the list actually used. After the first salvo, it is good strategy to list the words not yet eliminated by the crash pattern, and
tailor the next salvo to minimize the maximum number of words to
be guessed subsequently.

One trap to watch out for, especially in Wild Crash, is a target
word ending in -IGHT, which has ten first-letter possibilities in the
Pocket Dictionary. To protect against this, these ten initial letters
should be used in early test words as much as possible. -OUND is
a similar problem, but it has only eight alternatives to contend with.

In the five-letter Jotto variant of Crash, much effort has been put
into finding 5 five-letter words that contain 25 different letters of the
alphabet to use as an initial set of test words. However, a fairly large
dictionary is needed to accomplish this: FUDGY, JAMBS, PHLOX,
WRECK, QVINT in Webster's Second Unabridged, or CHUNK, VIBEX,
FJORD, GYMPS, WALTZ in Chambers Twentieth Century Dictionary.

Jotto is known as Secret Word by NOST members, and has been
played by them for at least ten years. For the seven-letter Jotto
variant, Garry Crum tries to select a test word which, as far as
possible, has a 33 per cent probability of having (1) one, (2) two,
or (3) zero or three or more hits with a randomly-chosen target.
As it is very tedious to check out the hit distributions of various words,
he suggests a quicker approximate method for evaluating a test word:
(1) for the first occurrence of each letter in the word, calculate the
percentage of possible target words which have this letter (this can
be done beforehand for each letter of the alphabet, and need not be repeated); (2) if the word has a repeated letter, similarly calculate the
percentage of possible target words that have this letter twice;
(3) add up these seven percentages. A good test word should have a
score of 175 or so. After the first three guesses, a better narrowing
of possibilities is sometimes obtained by aiming at 2 and 3 (or 3 and
4) hits instead of merely 1 and 2; for these, percentage sums of 260
(or 350) are recommended by Garry.

If Uncrash is played with five-letter words, players soon find that
the same words are used again and again. To introduce some variety
into this variant, Creede Lambard suggests (in the November 1976
NOST-Algia) that any word from five to nine letters long be accepted
as long as it can be fitted into a set of nine columns with the central
five columns all occupied; the crashing is judged only on the letters
in the central five columns, which no longer need be words.

The Game of Convergence, originally devised by members of the
Mathematical Research Department of Bell Labs at Murray Hill, N.J.
in the 1950s, is simply Crash with words substituted for letters and
additional information provided for non-crashes. Some sort of "halv-
ing" procedure seems best, starting with a mid-dictionary test sentence like LOATHSOME LOBBYIST LOCATES LOBELIAS.

SINKO

Description: In this symmetric two-person game, one player writes down a word of five letters in a five-by-five grid; the second player writes down a second five-letter word in parallel with the first, or adds four letters to one of the letters in the first word to form a five-letter word perpendicular to the first.   Players continue by adding words to the grid, on each move completing a word on one of the ten lines (five rows, five columns).   The winner is the last player who is able to add a word to the grid.

Variations: (1) To make this an n-person game, supply each player with his own grid.   The first player calls out a letter, and each player decides where to enter it on his grid.   Letters are called out in turn by all of the players until the grids have been filled.   A five-letter word in a row or column is scored 10 points, a four-letter word (if no five-letter one exists) is scored 5 points, and a three-letter word (if n four- or five-letter ones exist) is scored 3 points.   The winner is the player with the largest number of points (Score Words, Think of a Letter, Word Squares).

The game of Sinko was described by Dave Silverman in the May 1970 Word Ways.   The variation game was described in the September 1972, August 1973 and December 1973 issues of Games & Puzzles, but has apparently been known for a long time (see Eric Solomon's Games with Paper and Pencil).

The best strategy for Sinko is not known.   If both players are equally able, it has been noted that there seems to be a strong advantage in going second.   This is consistent with the following strategy: (1) if possible, place a word parallel to the first word such that no perpendicular word can be formed in any of the five available positions (the game will then end after four moves, with the second player winning); (2) if this is not possible, place a word parallel to the first word which allows perpendicular words to be formed in exactly two positions.   (After the opponent fills in one of these words, it may be possible to select the second word to block all further play.)   The best way for the first player to counter this strategy is to start with a word which is compatible with a large number of potential perpendicular words in all positions; words with rare letters should be avoided, as it makes the strategy given above easier to execute.

THE OILERS

Description: In this symmetric two-person game, the stockpile of allowed words is APE, BUD, CAN, DAY, DIE, DOT, HOP, LIP, ONE, PUT, RAT, RIG, ROW, RUE, SUN and TIN.   Each player in turn draws a word from the stockpile.   The first player wins if he obtains four words with no letters in common before the second player does; the second player wins if he obtains four words with no letters in common before the first player does, or if neither one succeeds in this endeavor.

This game was first described by Dave Silverman in the May 1972 Word Ways. A simplification of Norton Black's game of Euler Squares, it is uninteresting if both players know the optimum strategy, but may entertain those who do not.

The second player can guarantee a win by ensuring that neither player draws four words with no letters in common. To see this, consider the array of the sixteen words given at

day	one	put	rig
rue	lip	can	dot
tin	bud	row	ape
hop	rat	die	sun

the right: the twelve winning combinations are represented by the words forming the rows, the columns, the main diagonals, the corners, and the central square. Garry Crum devised a simple pairing strategy for the second player based on the above diagram. Allowing for symmetry, the first player has three opening moves: corner, side, or center. In the diagrams below, X represents the first player's opening move and O, the second player's response. The remaining fourteen cells are labelled from one to seven in pairs. After the initial exchange, the second player always chooses a cell labelled with the same number as that of first player's most recent selection. It can be clearly seen that each of the twelve four-word sets either contains the second player's O or else two cells of the same label.

```
X 6 5 O     7 X 7 1     1 3 5 5
4 1 5 4     4 0 3 2     2 X O 4
7 3 1 3     4 5 5 2     2 6 6 4
7 6 2 2     1 6 3 6     7 3 7 1
```

Thus the second player blocks every four-word set.

THE FOREHEAD GAME

Description: In this symmetric n-person game, each one of the players writes a four-letter word on a slip of paper. Each player then scotch tapes the paper to the forehead of the player on his right. Each player sees the words of all of his opponents but not his own. In turn, the players must announce a word with one letter taken from each of their opponents' words, or else he must take a guess at his own word. If he guesses his word (or a transposal of it) he wins; if he misses, he is ousted but his word remains on the table. No word or transposal thereof may be announced more than once.

This game works best with four, five or six people. There are at least three occasions when a player should take a stab at his own word: (1) when he reaches a point (owing to the poor play of an opponent) when he knows all his letters; (2) when he is no longer able to announce a word likely to appear in the agreed-upon dictionary; (3) when the only announcement he can think of will put an opponent into the first situation.

The skill factor in this game is largely in the choice of word announcements. Obviously, letters that appear in only one opponent's word should be avoided as long as possible. As for the choice of your right-hand opponent's word, it is good practice to give him repeated letters and a rare word to boot. This game was introduced by Dave Silverman in the November 1974 Word Ways.

ARROW OF LETTERS

Description: In this symmetric two-person game, players prepare
for the game by alternately writing down different letters until a
four-letter word has been formed. Arrows are then drawn from the
first letter to the second, from the second to the third, and from the
third to the fourth. Starting with this basic directed network of letters and arrows, each player in turn adds another letter (not previously used) together with additional arrows from one letter to
another as needed to spell out one or more words that read correctly
along the arrows. Restrictions on arrow-construction and word-
formation are: (1) no letter can have more than four arrows attached
to it (by point or flight) ; (2) if an arrow goes from letter A to letter
B, no arrow can subsequently be drawn from B to A; (3) no arrow
may cross another (that is, the graph must be planar) ; (4) all
words claimed by a player on his turn must include the letter he has
added to the network on that turn; (5) a player cannot claim both a
word and another word contained in it (as WHEAT and HEAT) ;
(6) no letter can be claimed more than once in a word. The game
ends when no one can make any additional moves; the score for a
player is the total number of letters in all the words he has formed.

This game was devised by Michael Grendon and published in the
December 1975 Games & Puzzles magazine. It is played by members
of NOST.

WORD BATTLESHIPS

Description: In this asymmetric two-person game, the first player
writes down a short well-known saying or proverb in the squares of
an n-by-n grid, each successive letter being entered in an adjacent
square (up, down, right or left) and spaces between words ignored.
The second player attempts to ascertain the saying by naming
squares one at a time in the grid; each time he names a square, he
is told its contents (a named letter or a blank). Each time he adds
a square, he can also attempt to guess the saying that has been par-
tially revealed; the game ends when his guess is correct. His score
is determined by adding the number of blank squares he hit to the number of letters in the message which he did not hit (but correctly
guessed).

This game was devised by David Parlett and published in Games &
Puzzles magazine in February 1976. Usually, a five-by-five grid is
about the right size to use.

FICTIONARY DICTIONARY

Description: In this asymmetric n-person game, one player selects
a dictionary word whose meaning is unknown to the others, and writes
its definition down on a slip of paper. The other players write down
invented definitions on slips of paper, and the first player collects
the slips and reads them off in random order (including his own).
Each player votes on the definition that he believes to be the correct

one. Each player (other than the first player) earns a point if he
picks the correct definition, plus an additional point each time one
of the others selects his false definition. The game is played until
each player in turn has had a chance to select a dictionary word.

Variations: (1) The first player selects a sentence from a book
(preferably a novel rather than a dictionary) of eight words or less,
and announces the name of the book and the initial letters of the
words (in order). Each of the other players writes a sentence
with words using the same initial letters in the same order, and
the voting and scoring proceeds as before (Suspended Sentences).
(2) Instead of announcing the set of initial letters of the words in
the sentence, the first player announces the lengths of the words
in the sentence (in order).

Also known as the Lexicographer's Game, this was reported in
Games & Puzzles for November 1973, February 1976 and April 1976.
It was brought to the attention of Gyles Brandreth by Mary Archer,
an academic at Oxford University. The first variation was devised
by David Parlett. Although this game requires a bit more than
pencil and paper, it can still be played in many environments.

The skill of this game lies in the invention of etymologies which
the other players find plausible, in accurately reproducing the phras-
ing and style of the dictionary in use, and in spotting turns of speech
or habits of thought that give opponents away. The first one to vote
can sometimes profitably bluff by choosing his own definition -- it
is worth a lot more to have the others follow your lead than to chance
a correct guess. Even the first player can bluff, by selecting a word
with a definition resembling the habits of thought of one of the players.

LAST WORD

Description: In this symmetric n-person game, a nine-by-nine grid
of squares is drawn on a sheet of paper, and the central nine
squares filled in with a random series of letters from text. Each
player in turn adds a letter in a square adjacent (right, left, up or
down) to a letter played earlier. Using this newly-placed letter,
plus letters that are in line with it either vertically, horizontally or
diagonally, words are formed by transposition; thus, if D is placed
in line with OWO, the word WOOD can be formed. Restrictions on
word-formation: (1) the letters to be transposed must form a continuous sequence, uninterrupted by unused letters or blank spaces;
(2) only one word can be claimed in each direction; (3) at least
two directions must form words. The game is scored by multiplying
the lengths of the words formed on each turn, and adding scores from
different turns. It terminates when a letter has been placed in at
least one square along each of the four edges of the layout.

Variation: Each player is given the alphabet to use, and crosses off
each of his letters that he adds to the pattern. The winner is the
first one to use all his letters or, if everyone is blocked, the one
that has the fewest letters left. The grid can be extended as needed.

This game, invented by Sid Sackson and reported in his book A Gamut of Games published in 1969, appeared in the September 1975 issue of Games & Puzzles magazine. It has been played by members of NOST for several years.

BLACK SQUARES

Description: In this symmetric two-person game, a twelve-by-twelve grid of squares is drawn on a sheet of paper. The first player places one (or more) letters anywhere on the grid, with the restriction that any sequence of adjacent letters, read to the right or down, must be a word or imbeddable in a word that can be fitted within the grid. The second player attempts to designate one or more of the squares of the grid "black squares" -- ones that cannot be filled by any letter which can (with other letters added, if necessary) be incorporated into a word joining the existing layout. If he is unable to find a black square, he must add one or more letters to the grid under the restrictions given above, and his opponent looks for black squares. The two players alternate in this fashion until the grid is filled or further progress blocked. Each player scores one point for each black square he fills in, and two points if he successfully challenges his opponent's black square by filling in letters joining it to the existing layout.

This game was first described by Harry Woollerton in the November 1975 Games & Puzzles.

WORD PING-PONG

Description: In this symmetric two-person game, players alternately convert a four-letter word to another four-letter word by changing one letter, subject to the restrictions that (1) the server (the player who initiates the series) can change only the first or second letters, and his opponent can change only the third or fourth letters; (2) no letter can be used more than three times in a given position in the words in a series; (3) the first word in a series must be convertible to another word by the opponent; (4) no word can be used more than once in a series. The last player who can convert a word to another word wins a point, and a new series is then initiated. Service changes after five points have been scored, and the first person to reach 21 points is the winner.

Variation: In this symmetric n-person game, the server writes down a four-letter word. Each player in turn converts the word presented to him into another word by changing one letter, subject to the conditions that (1) a player cannot change either of the two letters introduced by the two previous players; (2) no letter can be used more than five times in a given position. The first player who cannot add to the chain scores a demerit, and service passes to the next player in turn. When a player has accumulated a specified number of demerits, he is eliminated from the game; the last survivor is the winner.

This game was invented by P. Perkins and introduced in Games & Puzzles in December 1976.

PI

Description: In this symmetric two-person game, players alternately add letters to an n-by-n grid. The loser is the player who has to
break one of the following rules applicable to each row and each column: (1) three or more adjacent letters form a word; (3) the letters
in any row or column are such that no word of two or more letters
can be formed by subsequent additions of suitable letters. Players
can challenge the legitimacy of each other's moves; the loser of a
challenge loses the game at once (as in Ghost).

Pi was invented by John Shepherd of NOST, and first reported in
NOST-Algia in July 1976. Grid sizes ranging from five-by-five to
eight-by-eight have been proposed.

TEN LOGOTOPIAN LINGOS

Most people are familiar with Pig Latin (Amscray, the Opscay!) as a secret language. J. A. Lindon of Weybridge, Surrey, England has raised the construction of secret languages to a high art. Ten varieties are given below. Of these, the first, Palindromian, is perhaps the best-known, as it has been featured in both Howard Bergerson's Palindromes and Anagrams (Dover, 1973) and Martin Gardner's "Mathematical Games" in the February 1977 Scientific American magazine.

1. Palindromian

IN EDEN, I

Adam: Madam --
Eve: Oh, who --
Adam: (No girl-rig on!)
Eve: Heh?
Adam: Madam, I'm Adam.
Eve: Name of a foeman?
Adam: O stone me! Not so.
Eve: Mad! A maid I am, Adam.
Adam: Pure, eh? Called Ella? Cheer up.
Eve: Eve, not Ella. Brat-star ballet on? Eve.
Adam: Eve?
Eve: Eve, maiden name. Both sad in Eden? I dash to be manned,
       I am Eve.
Adam: Eve. Drowsy baby's word. Eve.
Eve: Mad! A gift. I fit fig, Adam . . .
Adam: On, hostess? Ugh! Gussets? Oh, no!
Eve: ? ? ?
Adam: Sleepy baby peels.
Eve: Wolf! Low!
Adam: Wolf? Fun, so snuff 'low'.
Eve: Yes, low. Yes, nil on, no linsey-wolsey.
Adam: Madam, I'm Adam.
       Named under a ban,
       A bared, nude man ---
             Aha!

Eve: Mad Adam!
Adam: Mmmmmmmmm!
Eve: Mmmmmmmmm!
Adam: Even in Eden I win Eden in Eve.
Eve: Pure woman in Eden, I win Eden in -- a mower-up!
Adam: Mmmmmmmmm!
Eve: Adam, I'm Ada.
Adam: Miss, I'm Cain, a monomaniac. Miss, I'm --
Eve: No, son.
Adam: Name's Abel, a male, base man.
Eve: Name not so, O stone man!
Adam: Mad as it is, it is Adam.
Eve: I'm a Madam Adam, am I?
Adam: Eve?
Eve: Eve mine. Denied, a jade in Eden, I'm Eve.
Adam: No fig. (Nor wrong if on!)
Eve: ? ? ?
Adam: A daffodil I doff, Ada.
Eve: 'Tis a -- what -- ah, was it --
Adam: Sun ever. A bare Venus . . .
Eve: 'S pity! So red, ungirt, rig-nude, rosy tips . . .
Adam: Eve is a sieve!
Eve: Tut-tut!
Adam: Now a seesaw on . . .
Eve: On me? (O poem!) No!
Adam: Aha!
Eve: I won't! O not now, I --
Adam: Aha!
Eve: NO! O God, I -- (Fit if I do?) Go on.
Adam: Hrrrrrh!
Eve: Wow! Ow!
Adam: Sores? (Alas, Eros!)
Eve: No, none. My hero! More hymen, on, on . . .
Adam: Hrrrrrrrrrrrrrrh!
Eve: Revolting is error! Resign it, lover.
Adam: No, not now I won't. On, on . . .
Eve: Rise, sir!
Adam: Dewy dale, cinema-game . . .   nice lady wed?
Eve: Marry an Ayr ram!
Adam: Rail on, O liar!
Eve: Live devil!
Adam: Diamond-eyed no-maid!
Both: Mmmmmmmmmmmm!

2. Dodecanian

In his <u>Nineteen Eighty-Four</u>, George Orwell forgot to mention Dodecania, that tiny, inaccessible state, nominally in the Oceanian sector of the tripartite globe, but left semi-autonomous on account of the difficulties of properly subjecting it. As the price of their outward conformity the Dodecanians make quiet fun of their huge jack-booted neighbour. Their private version of Newspeak, for example, boils the language down to a mere twelve words per subject, as in the Miniluv idiom, exemplified below, where characteristically the word is used in a sense very different from Oceania's.

In the Miniluv idiom, the twelve essential words are

I	doll	meet	not
U	fella	luv	
	tempa	bed	
	squalla	chop	
		quit	

Position in sentence indicates whether subject or object. First person plural is UI. Prefixing of nouns or pronouns indicates possession, hyphened repetition indicates emphasis or plurality.   An example:

I meet U. I luv U. UI bed. Squalla.
I luv squalla, U not-luv squalla.
Squalla tempa, U tempa, I tempa.
U chop squalla, squalla not-squalla.
I quit U, meet fella, luv fella, bed fella. Squalla.
I luv squalla, fella not-luv squalla.
Squalla tempa, fella tempa, I tempa.
Fella quit I, meet doll, luv doll, bed doll. Squalla.
Squalla tempa, fella tempa, doll tempa, fella quit doll.
I meet doll, doll tempa, I tempa, I-squalla tempa, doll-squalla
    tempa, TEMPA-TEMPA-TEMPA . . .
                <u>luv</u>!

3. Frascarian

The name derives from <u>phrases carrees</u>, square sentences.
There are two main dialects, the very limited one spoken by the Purists, in which every utterance is a genuine word-square, and the more flexible lingo of the Mixians, who allow words to overrun freely. Thus a Mixian might say: "Follow on, loyal nag," which forms an overrunning sentence-square as shown at the right. A couple of examples will make the matter clear.

F O L L
O W O N
L O Y A
L N A G

(a) Purist Dialect

X: Was Ada sad?
Y: She had Eda.
X: Yes, Eda saw.
Y: Saw Ada was --
X: Too old. Odd.
Y: It's the sea.
X: It's the sex.
Y: His ice -- sex?
X: Was age sea?
Y: Age? God! Eda.
X: Rae and Eda.
Y: Was Ada sad!

(b) Mixian Dialect

Cheerful Barber: Good old mod madman!
Customer: Good morn! "Noon's End" next month.
Cheerful Barber: Nuts! Up on top I snip?
Customer: Not too short -- head-to-axe order.
Cheerful Barber: Any snip-type . . . -- a stab?
Customer: Wow! Ow! Away!
Cheerful Barber: No blood, Abdulla. Lo!
Customer: Fool! Dolt! Spot, boil . . . -- sound pint!
Cheerful Barber: (Half a gill is a flap!)
   (Noon's End is presumably the title of some film or show)

4. Nosetailian

Once again, a language with several dialects, all deriving from ordinary English words by the tender-before-engine process of formation. In the Mercerian Straits, Choptic Latin is spoken:

Intra bella pireum vivere,
Barum covitemus, edus belli temptat,

while in the Nimmerlander of Lindonia, Nosetailian Deutsch is more
commonly met with:

Alle ableten Redlinge schicken Ausbure einher,
Dahil ist eidner Zolben gemanbar gelozen.

There is even one tiny, but highly progressive community, that of the

Neocyclics, in which the pure <u>lingua nuova</u> is in everyday use:

Piase dowsha vero engre dowmea.

Two dialects which use quasi-English words are much more widely spoken than any of the above, and so have far greater importance. Nosetailia was originally colonised by settlers from Transposia, and the first of these dialects, Tanglean, bears a close resemblance to the mother tongue. Only a sprinkling of genuine Nosetailian words occur (cf. George Orwell's semi-Newspeak of 1984), but the Tangleans insist that both these words and their English roots make some kind of sense in the context. In what follows, the Nosetailian words are underlined.

(a) Example of Tanglean Dialect

Ralfe: <u>Dy-how</u>?
Gerti: <u>O-hell</u>! (Ideas) <u>Vocha</u>, you <u>shooy</u>!
Ralfe: A <u>callo</u> girl can be <u>yallo</u>. Don't let the boys <u>arest</u> you out.
Gerti: (seeing the <u>micco</u> side): <u>Gueton</u>, you wag! Be like the <u>onest</u>.
Ralfe: (<u>ernst</u>): Don't start raising your <u>bowel</u>.
Gerti: And drink <u>coaco</u>? A <u>cofi</u> for that! I need something more
       like <u>cida</u>.
Ralfe: You <u>chatta</u> no importance to our <u>Valri</u>?
Gerti: She's <u>tricci</u>, I grant you. Oh, but that <u>letcha</u> is <u>al-fat</u>!
Ralfe: Your wit is <u>catti</u>. Still, she's no <u>nyti</u>.
Gerti: I've known her <u>ly-bare ancle</u>.
Ralfe: We are two in <u>Essex</u>. You can <u>glean</u> for the rest.
Gerti: Well, stay <u>veali</u>!
Ralfe: <u>In-scoff</u> to you!

The second of our two important dialects which use quasi-English words is Novanglian. This lingo, which is composed entirely of Nosetailian words and is now spoken throughout the whole of Mercedonia, may be regarded as the standard form of the language. It resembles Numbo-Carrean in many ways (see Section 7), although its origins are different and there are no strict word-endings, e.g., English <u>Lethe</u>, <u>callus</u>, <u>heron</u> give 'He-let us-call on-her'.

(b) Novanglian (Nosetailian proper)

IN-THE DINE-'AL

L: O-deer, I-can't fech-a laga to-Gus or-an ale-more to-Len!
M: Wy-the 'ot-hel 'Ary-not?

L: O-Maxi, I-pot-pourr al-term-in getting-for Teries-lot.
M: Sech-a slav-yu-go and-comm?
L: Ewan, 'e-ses-I-am.
M: Ewan? O-punch-in-'ell! He's-a-pac of-'oli 'orers!
L: He-let me-tire-so much-in-so long-a table-time.
M: Tanks nede there-ale.
L: U-men! Like-a cofi?
M: My-rum, Lidea.

5. Spoonerian

A: Hot woe, Barley Chinks!
B: Hot woe, Chilly Base!
A: Blocking showy, Miss Thorning.
B: Glowing a bale.
A: It slacked one of my crates.
B: I've a late slacking. The drain rips in.
A: Porter on the willows? Tut-tut!
B: Mad for the bite. Cuddles on the pot.
A: A very washy splinter.
B: All blood and mowing.
A: Here's to spray in the Ming!
B: Sadsome glummer! 'Ware fell!
A: Low song!

6. Transposian

A: Do gong Minor!
B: Moon-dog grin!
A: I saw your drug-hate in town stay reedy.
B: The guard? What was she on dig, I'd like to wonk?
A: She had a moany gnu with her.
B: The boy's lost! I'll give her a rash thing for this.
A: High rants? Oh, let the girl be, it's only Alan Rut.
B: I've said she must let us know before she starts to lug a wink.
A: Perhaps you're girth.
B: Seedy tray, you said. That would be Diary F.
A: No, no! A dust-ray.
B: Ah, yes, of course. Rusty Ada. Should have been at her
      minus closes. She'll get bristles on her sick bead for
      this, you see if she dents-O!
A: (emu-sad) That's not I, Kelly, old man! Well, it's your
      sin buses, I've my own tram-set to think of. Slog on!
B: No logs.

7. <u>Numbo-Carrean</u>

For a fuller, but still very incomplete account of this entertaining language, see Joseph S. Madachy's <u>Recreational Mathematics Magazine</u> for October 1962 (issue no. 11). Suffice it to say here that every word in Numbo-Carrean, whether simple or compounded of hyphened or apostrophized parts, is such that, if its letters be replaced by their alphabet position numbers, a square number results. Thus, in the dialogue below, the patient's name, Burti D'Feld, gives the two squares 22118209 and 465124, which can be found from a table of squares without any need for calculation.

Af d Medigfa

Cicbedda: Doc'ddd Yocif H.
 Bedli?
Medigfa: Iuf, libbe d doc'ddd.
 Iulbe cicli? Nam'dd --
C: Burti D'Feld. libbe cyxti,
 a ryta. Iuf, live d ed-fau,
 ed-evy, tad-badd, bihap I goh-
 heu rheli goefy. libbe anx'd.

M: Ar-ha. Yiu haf-a-cof?
C: Hikcf! Hikcf! Hikcf! Yiu
 cee-I-cof. Hikcf!
M: I erd. I gheqcu up. Cudhi..
 ar-ha.. ar-ha.. miidhi...

C: Ou!
M: 'Scu! Aic-dhha? Sawli?
 Side-of d ribbe be oditif.
 Miidhi.. Oli Staix! Yiu be
 odd-eer'd!
C: (anx'd) 'Zbadd? T'be
 odd-eer'd?
M: Yiu awta ly up, be abedd,
 have a wecof, yiu be a cic-
 bedda.
C: Whi-bedd? 'Zgodlove! I
 shha di? Al-up-di? DDDDDD-
 HHHHHI?
M: (fceti) Stiif. Cohdd. Icly
 bleu cohdd. Me-give up,
 cas-bbbe ahszadd, a-nazdhi --
C: Aydd! Aiddha! By Ghgawhd,

At the Doctor's

Patient: Doctor Joseph H.
 Bedley?
Medico: Yes, I'm the doctor.
 You're unwell? Name --
P: Bertie Fields. I'm sixty, a
 writer. Yes, my head's funny,
 feels sort of swollen, as if I
 were a tadpole, maybe I'm
 going plumb crazy. I'm worried.

M: Ah-ha. You have a cough?
P: Hough! Hough! Hough! You
 see I cough. Hough!
M: I heard. I'll give you a
 check-up. Could I.. ah-ha..
 ah-ha.. might I...

P: Ow!
M: Sorry! Pain there? Much?
 One side of your ribs is funny.
 Might I.. Holy mutton! Your
 ears don't match!
P: (nervously) Is that bad?
 To have odd ears?
M: You ought to lie up, be abed,
 have a week off, you're an in-
 valid.
P: Why bed? For the love of
 Moses! I shall die? All up --
 die? DDDDIIIIIIIIIEE?
M: (facetiously) Stiff. Cold. Icy
 blue cold. I give up, the case
 is very sad, a nasty --
P: Help! Oh, help! By crikey,

Iive need've yiu, ang-yeu! I
ha v'ta be aliifi --
M: Phhchha! Be hush'dd! I
   aide-fiu. Yiu be a ryta, yiu
   have atac-of fame-aigu, sohli
   d fame-aigu, neggax, nigfi!
   I mix yiu up d medx, yiu netbe
   pha d nhiif. Varti.. ar-ha..
   ar-ha.. sfxi! D cicbedda
   taixa kwhata ofy d mixhchef,
   Medx P XXXI, affda mili.
   Guht-af!

C: Guht-af!
M: Oeyp! Fe-give.
C: Yhhhha!

I've need of you, blow you! I
have to be alive, I --
M: Fcha! Be quiet! I help a
   few. You're a writer, you
   have an attack of fame-fever,
   it's only fame-fever, nothing
   much, it's not serious! I'll
   mix you up some medicine,
   you're not for the operating-
   table. Wait now.. ah-ha.. ah-
   ha.. that's it! The patient
   takes a quarter of the mixture,
   Potion P 31, after meals.
   Good-afternoon!

C: Good-afternoon!
M: Oips! My fee.
C: Yah!

8. Liquidian

Laura: You were aware early, Will.
Will: I worry, Laura. I worry o'er our Wally.
Laura: Our Wally? Away wi' you! We worry o'er you, Will.
Will: Wally, a raw wooer, a real worry, Laura.
Laura: Leery Lily, eh? A low lolly-lurer!
Will: Yeah. Lily will wilily lure our oily Wally.
Laura: Oh, you err, Will!
Will: Wryly I allow lolly, I rue, I weary, I weigh Wally, I
        worry. Early I worry, all Yule I worry, all year
        I worry. A rare worry, our Wally.
Laura: You owe your Wally a loyal role, Will.
Will: Oh, well, we're aware. I'll really, Laura, really I will.
Laura: You lie, Will. You're a liar, you ol' roue!

9. Explodian

This language uses only the explosive consonants -- the hard
sounds of b, c(k), d, g, p and t -- and the short vowels, as in the
sentence 'that pen is not much good'.

Dick: Good egg!
Dot: Good duck!
Dick: Get Teddy to pick up a bucket o' cod, Dot.
Dot: Teddy 'ud pick a pocket, but duck a bucket o' cod, Dick.
       Got a bucket o' cod to pick up?
Dick: Daddy got it, Bob added a titbit, Betty gutted it. Got to

g et it to Biddy to cook.
Dot: Teddy -- a giddy cub, a tot, a tag-puppet, a pick-up-ticket
               pocketed-pegtop oddity? A pity to add a bucket to a
               tip-up kid! Get big Paddy to pick it up, Dick.
Dick: Good tactic! Paddy copied a caddie, took a puppy to Peggy,
               a buddy to back, bedad!
Dot: A pukka cadet! Uppa deck, Dick!
Dick: Top attic, Dot!

10. <u>Newspeak</u>

    Orwell repeatedly mentions Newspeak in <u>Nineteen Eighty-Four</u>
and even devotes an appendix to the language, but when the relevant
information is collected and examined, it is found to be pretty slen-
der. I think only one three-word sentence is actually given. The
following extended passage must therefore be regarded only as giving the general idea. It purports to be part of the 1984 <u>Definitive
Edition of Shakespeare</u> in Newspeak as rewritten by the poet Amble-
forth. No wonder he was vaporized!

          HAMLET unduckspeakwise:

                Person or unperson. Query.
Unbellyfeel Ingsoc, oldthink, ownthink,
(PLUSUNGOOD THOUGHTCRIME. PENALTY:
               UNLIFE)
Or Ingsoc foolthink doubleplusungood,
Own unlife bellyfeel, make self unlifer,
Unperson, unofficial. (PENALTY: JOYCAMP)
Only unwake: become unlifer. (FOOLTHINK)
Unwake, and thusby unperform our Ingsoc duty
(GOODWISE NOTE: BIG BROTHER IS WATCHING
 YOU) seems goodthink (DOUBLEPLUSUNGOOD
THOUGHTCRIME). Unwake: become unlifer.
Unwake -- ungoodwise dream (PLUS-CERTAINFUL
SELF-BRINGED RESULT) --
Yes, there is the unsmoothness --
Correctful treatment in the Miniluv,
Post fail-maked self unlifer with a cord,
Is allsuch stopful -- yes, there is the reason
We still goodwise perform our Ingsoc duty
Until we're vaporized, although (CRIMETHINK)
Unbellyfeeling Ingsoc and Big Brother,
The Junior Anti-Sex League, rationed goods,
Sternness of Inner Party and its just
And ungood 'watch and query' note on us,

We seemcould oldthink 'free' perhaps become
With a bigneedle. (FOOLTHINK) Who would work,
Prolewise and sweatful, doubleplusunfresh,
For Ingsoc if he bellyfeeled to know
Correctful treatment in the Miniluv
That joyful place from which so few return,
And those how bigwise changed? Plusgooderwise
We live goodthinkful til some Spy reports us,
For IGNORANCE is STRENGTH, FREEDOM is
                    SLAVERY,
And WAR (against the Party) brings NO PEACE
Inside the Miniluv till we become
Unpersons (now OFFICIAL).
                                    But unhard!
The clingful and face-crimewise-good-to-see
Ophelia! Joysexful girl, forget
My many faults in your Two Minutes Hate!

THE LAST WORD

What is the last word in the dictionary? This seemingly-simple question has been the subject of endless debate, involving its participants in perplexing discussions as to what constitutes a "word" and what does not. The conservative approach to the question is to look in various contemporary large English-language dictionaries:

American Heritage: Zyzzyva, a genus of tropical American
     weevils
Webster's Third: Zyzzogeton, a genus of South American leaf
     hoppers
Funk & Wagnalls: Zyzzle, to make a sputtering or hissing sound
Random House: Zyrian, a Uralic language

The Oxford English Dictionary, a considerably older reference work, offers zyxt, an obsolete version of "see". It will be interesting to see if this word is bettered in the four-volume Supplement currently being prepared.

Zzxjoanw

What about words in specialized dictionaries? If one rejects zzz (in the Random House Unabridged) or zzzz (in L. V. Berry and Melvin Van den Bark's The American Thesaurus of Slang (Crowell, 1953)) as onomatopoeic representations, as sounds of indefinite length rather than words, a leading candidate for the last word is ZZXJOANW, a weird collection of letters first appearing in Rupert Hughes' Music-Lovers Encyclopedia in 1914. This word was accepted without comment for more than 60 years, until Philip Cohen of Aliquippa, Pennsylvania took a closer look at its entry:

zzxjoanw (shaw) Maori. 1. Drum 2. Fife. 3. Conclusion.

Commenting on this in the November 1976 issue of Word Ways:

There are a number of odd points here: the pronunciation, homonymous with 'pshaw' and little related to the spelling; the strange diversity of meanings; and the curious appropriateness of 'conclusion' as the last meaning of the last entry in the dictionary section. (Could 'drum' and 'fife' convey something, too?) But the clincher comes when we look at Maori. A typical sentence, from Harawira's Teach Yourself Maori, is "Ataahua ana ki te titiroatu". Maori has no closed syllables or consonant clusters, let alone the conglomerations of 'zzxjoanw', nor even an 's' or 'sh' sound. The available Maori dictionaries give words for 'drum' and 'end', but they haven't the slightest resemblance to 'zzxjoanw' or 'shaw'.

A hoax clearly entered somewhere. It's not certain where, since Hughes cites no sources, but I suspect it began and ended with him. (Could it be that he had a wife or a daughter named Joan? He was married three times.)   He probably intended the hoax to be obvious, but he reckoned without logologists, made credulous by experience with other outlandish words.

Whatever his motives, I, for one, feel betrayed. I thought that 'zzxjoanw' was the perfect example of an amazing-but-real word; there is no other one cockeyed enough to replace it. (A philosophi-co-logological question: does a hoax word gain legitimacy from 42 years' unchallenged appearance in a standard reference, and cita-tions elsewhere? An error, no, but 'zzxjoanw' approaches the status of a successful coinage -- successful, at least, among log-ologists.)

The message here is clear; odd words should not be uncritically ac-cepted, but every effort made to check their validity. If a citation of its usage is not provided, the logologist must surely feel uneasy until one is found. (To eliminate nonce-words, two or more citations are even better.)

Zzyzx Springs

What about place names? If these are allowed, a new candidate for the last word quickly appears. Pride of discovery must go to Dmitri Borgmann of Dayton, Washington, who prior to 1967 located this place name on a map of San Bernardino County, California, indicating a hydrologic feature and privately-owned spa about 8.5 miles south of Baker, on the western edge of Soda Dry Lake, off the abandoned right-of-way of the old Tonopah and Tidewater Railroad. It is listed simply as Zyzzx in both the 1973 Hammond Ambassador World Atlas and the 1976 Rand McNally Commercial Atlas and Marketing Guide, and has a population of 100. Further proof of the reality of this place name is provided by signs on a nearby interstate highway pointing to a Zzyzx Rd. exit.

Zzzzra

What about surnames in telephone directories or city directories? The last one known to occur in any telephone directory is Zachary Zzzzra, who has appeared in every edition of the San Francisco tele-phone directory since 1972. (His closest competitor is James Zzzzee, in the 1976 Manhattan directory.)   There are also a handful of three-Z names in recent directories:

Archimedes L Zzzyandottie, Manhattan 1972, 1973
Vladimir Zzzyd, Miami 1972, 1973, 1974
Budd(y) Zzzyp, Manhattan 1972, 1973, 1976
Zeke Zzzypt, Atlanta 1974
Robert Zzzypt, Miami 1973
Robert Zzzyzzitt, San Francisco 1972
Zebra Zulu Zzzyzzy, Jacksonville 1974

If a telephone subscriber says that his name is Zachary Zzzzra and wishes to be so listed, the telephone company is unlikely to challenge him to prove it. It seems likely that most, if not all, multiple-Z surnames were coined by the user merely for the notoriety of being last in the phone book, and are not used by their owners in any other situation. This supposition is strengthened by the fact that Zyzo is the last surname in Social Security records; there are six people bearing this surname in the United States, although no telephone directory entry has ever been found.

It is a bit hard to decide just when a surname should be admitted as a word having a genuine existence. To avoid frivolous inventions, it is desirable to insist that a surname must be regularly used by an individual in all of his business or social activities; better yet, the name should have been passed on from parent to child over two or more generations, or be used by individuals in several different localities.

Philip Cohen has pointed out that the only way to verify a telephone directory surname is to write or telephone its owner, asking for more information: the correctness of the spelling, the existence of other people bearing the name, and other references (such as newspapers or magazines) in which it can be found. He is probably correct, but people, unlike reference books, can lie or refuse to answer, feeling that information about their surname is nobody else's business. Those whose names are extremely unusual are likely to be especially uncooperative, having been pestered too often by inquiries from strangers.